A More Perfect Ten

Writing and Producing
the Ten-Minute Play

Gary Garrison

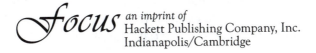 *an imprint of*
Hackett Publishing Company, Inc.
Indianapolis/Cambridge

A More Perfect Ten

© 2009 Gary Garrison

Focus an imprint of
Hackett Publishing Company

For further information, please address
Hackett Publishing Company, Inc.
P.O. Box 44937
Indianapolis, Indiana 46244-0937

www.hackettpublishing.com

Front cover image © istockphoto/ Cevdet Gökhan Palas
Back cover image © istockphoto/ Ahmet Dalkiliçlar

ISBN-13: 978-1-58510-327-0 (pbk.)

Printed in the United States of America

21 20 19 18 17   4 5 6 7 8 9

The paper used in this publication meets the minimum requirements of
American National Standard for Information Sciences—Permanence of
Paper for Printed Library Materials, ANSI Z39.48–1984.

Table of Contents

Acknowledgements

First and foremost, a special thanks goes to my editor at Heinemann, Lisa Barnett, for liking my first book enough to give me a second, and for believing that something as short as a ten-minute play deserves a whole book. Lisa, you left us a short while ago, but we miss you more with each passing day. Hope you found a good horse up there.

To Cathy Norgren, Gregg Henry and Jay Edelnant for allowing me to take to the wind and fly with it everywhere I went. BDG adores you all like no other.

To my colleague, co-producer and close friend, Maggie Lally, for suffering through producing one ten-minute play festival after another at NYU with me, and for never losing her sense of humor when I lost mine for the gazillionth time.

To my mentor and friend, Mark Dickerman, for the example he sets at NYU for all teachers and dramatists. Thanks for the free time when I announced, "I have to write."

To Michel Wallerstein, Matthew Rasenick, Lindsay Walker and Julie Maldonado, Ross Maxwell and Jayme McGhan for sharing your talent and your artistry in this book. Bravo.

To the good folks at Focus Publishing, especially Ron Pullins, for picking me up and putting me back in publication. It's always a pleasure to collaborate with you.

Finally, to all the playwrights that I've spoken to in a public forum about your work: I often had more to say about your play, but unfortunately not the time to say it. So I said what I thought you needed to hear. I know that a writer can never hear enough about their work, so what was left to say, I've said in this book. It's because of you that I wrote it. Thanks, from the bottom of my heart, for the inspiration.

A More Perfect Ten

Writing and Producing
the Ten-Minute Play

To my mom and dad, 'cause something should always
be dedicated to those who've helped you through
this life with love...

Introduction

Wait-a-minute-wait-a-minute! Wasn't there a book called Perfect Ten: Writing and Producing the Ten-Minute Play? – Uhhhh. Yeah. Yeah, there was, cowboy – *Wait-a-minute-wait-a-minute! Isn't a lot of this book the same book, only with a not-so-different title? –*

Uhhhh. Yep. True enough, cowgirl. There are a few considerable additions, but it's pretty much the same book – *Wait-a-minute-wait-a-minute! What the f? What gives?*

If you live long enough, you realize that most questions in life don't have easy answers, but this question's a piece of cake to answer. Heinemann Press published the original book back in 2000 and did a helluva job (they published four of my five books). Then, life and circumstances set in. My original editor, the inspired Lisa Barnett, passed away from this world way too early and Heinemann's drama division of books no longer had a leader, a visionary; there was no one to fight the good fight. Money got tight around Heinemann, resources got even tighter and before you know it, they were looking to sell off their drama division. But it never happened because a big ol' company stepped in and bought all of Heinemann. As you might guess, the big ol' new company wasn't too keen on keeping a drama division.

Enter the ever-energetic and all-around good guy, Ron Pullins, and the good folks at Focus Publishing. Literally within days of Heinemann being sold and graciously releasing its authors to find new publishers, Ron Pullins stepped in to offer a home for this book and others. I couldn't have been any happier and I'll tell you: I'd wanted to do a second edition of this book for a long damn time. I wanted to replace the plays in the original book with new, exciting material that I'd discovered over the last eight years, add a chapter on structure, update the submission opportunities, share more of the wisdom I've gleaned from writing and producing more ten-minute plays in eight years – well, essentially, bring it around to something even more meaningful and useful than the first edition. As my pierced and tatted godson would say, "Yeh, daawwg, s'all good."

This was from the original introduction to *Perfect Ten:*

I wouldn't be crazy enough to label this a "*How To* Write A Ten-Minute Play" book, but I will suggest that what follows is a brief guide for writing the newest form in theatre. If you're a playwright, consider this a primer for what makes good, compelling theatre and discover how that has no less a place in these little *hors d'oeuvre* dramas. If you're a theatre manager, director, or artistic director, we're going to look at the very real practicalities of producing ten-minute plays. We'll also examine six different writers' approaches in constructing a ten-minute play and discover how singularity of voice is every bit as true in a tightly constricted form. And last, you're going to write your own ten-minute play and explore it, dramaturgically, against the ideas presented in the book.

A word of caution: like all creative ventures, the process takes longer than the product. And that's a good thing. And don't take the title of the book wrong: I'm not trying to get you to write a perfect ten-minute play; I'm tying to perfect *you* writing a ten-minute play.

Gary Garrison,
New York City
October 2008

I appreciate the form most when it's really the only option that could possibly contain the experience the writer wishes to give the audience. I don't like it when I feel short-shrifted, when I'm left hungry for more. Or when the writer uses the form to tell a quick joke. I'd rather hear a quick joke while eating a Whopper Junior.

~ Gary Sunshine, playwright

Chapter 1

Bones for the Pickin'

We've created a monster and we don't even know it.

In the time it takes to sort through a pile of almost-white cotton socks from your dryer, whip up three eggs over-easy or watch George Bush try to explain some inane decision he's made, you could witness the newest double-edged sword the American theatre has to offer: the Ten-Minute Play. Look in any small to medium-sized theatre or educational institution across the country, and you're bound to smack right up against it. And it seems the trend is growing faster than anyone can keep up with.

Has it ever happened before that a generation of artists have embraced a new creative form with such wild energy and enthusiasm, completing whole, dramatic creations in the time it takes to languorously eat a slice of pepperoni pizza? I never even saw it coming. Did you? And where the heck did it come from? I wagered a guess in an article that I wrote for *The Dramatists Guild Newsletter* several years ago:

> First there was the full-length play about a ga-jillion years ago. Then some sassy, know-it-all playwright got daring (or maybe bored, or low on ink, or was a victim of attention deficit disorder) and thought, "why do in three long, <u>long</u> acts what you can do in one?" So the one-act play became the genre du jour until God created television and MTV. Then some clever playwright thought, "why do in one-act what you can do in ten-minutes or in a monologue play?" Shortly thereafter, God created Jane Martin and/or the Actors Theatre of Louisville, and the great submission flood rivaled its biblical equivalent. But sadly, pretty much every playwright's ten-minute play just died in the flood.
>
> So God created the *Dramatists Sourcebook and The DG Resource Directory*, and lo and behold, there appeared the One-Page Play. Wonder if God's going to create an audience for it? (If so, expect the next Great Flood). Pretty soon we'll have the No Page Play and

just a lot of playwrights lined up at the door of a literary manager who sits patiently listening to a writer say, "Just imagine a play…and it's really funny…"

…I shouldn't be surprised; none of us should: we are a generation of writers raised on television. We know the world in sound-bites and out-takes. Our television programming, commercials and films are doled out in fifteen-to-thirty-second images that flash only the condensation of emotion, with little screen time spent watching those emotions develop. We are used to an abbreviated expression of creativity. And I, as a teacher of playwriting, have to constantly work against that conditioning in the classroom, and then wrestle with it myself in my own creative soul…

Don't get me wrong, I like the ten-minute play. I'm a real sucker for it. I should be – every one I've written has been produced. But it wasn't enough that they be *my* creative best friend: I wanted *everybody* to love them. So I started a Ten-Minute Play Festival at NYU for the Dramatic Writing Program, another for my region of the Kennedy Center's American College Theatre Festival (which has now evolved into a national Ten-Minute Play Festival), another for Off-Off-Broadway's Pulse Ensemble Theatre, another for the Playwrights Program in the Association for Theatre in Higher Education and a few others that I've forgotten because the experience was…well, brief. I've championed the ten-minute play to my writer-friends and students for the last ten years as a new, exciting variation for the theatre – a writer's challenge, a great exercise for actors, a director's dream, a producer's profitable night at the box office.

That is until one day, several years ago, sitting in an Off-Off-Broadway theatre watching an evening of ten-minute plays that were really *bad*, really *long* and had about as much appeal as watching melted butter congeal, I recalled a healthy number of the four or five-hundred ten-minute plays I'd read, thought of all of those I had produced (about half that many)…and gulped a big, lugubrious gulp that most of Manhattan must have heard and that's still lodged in my throat. Why?

Because very few writers know what they're creating when they write them, what to do with them once they're written, and what to do with the skills they learn writing the short play when (and if) they finally sit down to write a long one. At the core of all of this is a very simple problem: few playwrights have thought about what these plays really are or what they should try to be and what magic (or disaster) they can create for their audience. Writers seem to universally acknowledge one thing: they're short, and it feels easier because *"how many mistakes can you make in such a short amount of time?"*

A lot. A load. Tons of them. So many you'd think you've never written a single word in your life. Shorter doesn't mean easier on any level. Ahhhhhhhhhh, there's the rub. Filling the "empty space" with evocative language, fascinating characters and a compelling story all in ten minutes is harder to write than any of us think, but we haven't spent much time thinking about it because it's all so new. Look, I know they're great fun to write, they're good learning tools for any writer, they're terrific acting and directing exercises and they're a fantastic way of introducing a large number of writers to an audience in one pop. BUT, there are very real, very solvable problems in the creation of this form that, if we just stop in our zealousness to create, we can solve with some good, sound dramaturgical thought in such a way that everyone wins. But before any of that can happen, I have to try to tackle my dread about the whole of it and pick a few bones with myself and the rest of the theatre world before encouraging anyone to write a ten-minute play.

BONE # 1
Right or Wrong, Short for Long

Call me reactionary, but I get scared when I see my art form shrinking with such wild abandon. I'm concerned that we're encouraging a new genre for a generation of writers not necessarily proficient or prolific in the long forms. I'm hesitant (but do it anyway) to teach my students how to write ten-minute plays when I know they haven't fully embraced the one-act play, let alone the full-length play. When I teach them the ten-minute play form, am I only reinforcing what ails them in the first place? And for myself, I'm afraid to keep writing ten-minute plays for fear of losing or dulling the fragile skills it's taken me years to learn writing the longer forms. The American theatre needs writers who can write full-length plays! Look on Broadway! We're not there! The Brits are there. And sometimes the Irish when they can elbow their way past the Brits. Everybody's pounding American dramatists into obscurity...and we're letting them.

And yet writing a ten-minute play is just so tempting because the whole thing is, well…it's so effin' short. In one afternoon, I can write a ten-minute play, do a thirty-pound load of wash, do a rewrite, water the dead plants, do another rewrite, paint my bathroom and be back at the computer to do a polish before the sun even thinks about going down. And believe or not, that scares me, if not for myself then other writers, because it *feels* easy. And if you've written long enough, you know nothing about it is easy and nothing about it is quick.

I can be at peace with this emerging form only if I make a commitment to use the same skills and creative know-how in writing the shorter form as with the long. And maybe that's where all of this goes awry. I mean, shouldn't the ten-minute play be some style of story driving dramatic action that has some sort of resolution and that lasts for ten minutes? It shouldn't be what amounts to just a scene or a Saturday Night Live sketch; it's probably not a monologue; definitely not a dance/poetry reading/choral ode to the universe's bio-system, but unfortunately, that's what I'm experiencing in the theatre when I see them time and again.

BONE #2
Short Means Thin

As I've traveled about the county, either through the Kennedy Center, the Dramatists Guild or by way of my own career as a writer and teacher, the number of bad ten-minute plays I've seen over the years has been enough to raise the dead (or at least, give 'em a good shake). I couldn't even say, "Well, at least they were only ten minutes," because the truth of the matter is few writers clock in on time. Several years ago I had the good fortune of traveling to eight different regions of the country as a member of a national response team for the Kennedy Center's American College Theatre Festival. Each region presented a ten-minute play festival, producing the work of college playwrights from their region. To my mind, what better circumstance could I find myself in that would illuminate the "state of the union" of this relatively new genre? Of the eighty or so ten-minute plays I saw or read, here's what I experienced, first by topic:

11 – I'm a boy, you're a girl, what's-the-difference-between-us?-oh-it's-just-under-standing-and/or-consensually-embracing-our-different-equipment play.

18 – I'm gay, you're gay, he's gay, she's gay, my roommate /father/mother/uncle/rabbi/doctor/dentist/lawyer/teacher/ mailman/pastor/therapist/accountant/massage therapist and-the-President-of-the-United-States-is-probably-gay play.

12 – The sex plays : I want to sex you if you want to sex me, but we really shouldn't be sexing because we're not really attracted to each other. Or, I sexed you when he wasn't looking, but you sexed him when you were looking right at me. So that's it. No more sexing…unless you want to. Truth is, I hate sex but what else can we do on a Friday night? – play.

15 – Saturday Night Live sketches-as-plays: the "what would happen if the world was suddenly overtaken by sponges" play? The "what would happen if men got pregnant instead of women?" play. Who's more important – Mr. Cheese or Mr. Cracker? The "arm-pits have feelings too" play.

8 – The "jump" plays: jumping centuries, jumping planets, jumping solar systems, jumping gender, jumping rope (believe it or not, not as bad you'd think), jumping realities, plains, levels, dimensions, personalities, diseases.

7 – The terrorist plays: anybody who was not Caucasian showed up in these plays with a chip on one shoulder and an Uzi on the other.

4 – The poetry plays; three were in iambic pentameter.

6 – The real thing: solid stories with conflict, character, sharp dialogue and a variety of structures in storytelling that was sometimes conventional, sometimes not.

Of these eighty plays, here's what I experienced in actual time: a third were *much longer* than ten-minutes, a third were *longer* than ten minutes and a third earned their classification. Bothersome? You bet. A ten-minute play should be ten minutes, or let's just call it a short play. And as for the sex-fest that dominated the subject matter of these plays, couldn't you make the argument that what I saw was highly appropriate to the age of the writer? Maybe, but good writing is good no matter the age and hormone surge. My issue with these plays was never the subject matter (though I often found it curious), but the thin, almost transparent and superficial treatment about issues of intimacy, gender identity, gender politics, sexuality, non-consensual sex, AIDS, racism, misogyny, cultural identity and so on. It takes extraordinary skill to write and develop a full-length play on any of these subjects. So you'd have to be a really good writer, nay, a PHENOMENAL writer to do justice to any of these subjects in a play that lasts for ten minutes.

BONE #3
A Writer's Arrogance

With a new genre that is constrained by an actual time factor (or number of pages) comes the challenge of trying to convince playwrights to learn the *art* or true skill of writing within its limitations and recognize that somebody down the line has to actually produce what's been written. A writer's arrogance will make him think that rules or restrictions never quite apply to his art, his masterpiece. And while I'm loathe to try to put any kind of standard, rule or aesthetic on a ten-minute play (what true writer would listen anyway?), there has to be some kind of substantive discussion, or, re-focusing on the genesis of good, involving drama for the sake of audience entertainment, no matter what its actual length of performance time. In other words, the real challenge here is to convince writers that the limitations in writing a ten-minute play should be a reason to become *more* creative, not less.

🔥 🔥 🔥

Wheewwww! Okay, I feel better. I just had to give a little voice to those reservations so that we can all start at square one together. Let's keep this in perspective: we're writing ten-minute plays, not discovering the origins of Black Holes. So if I screw my dramatist's head on right, what the ten-minute play should be is a self-contained story with compelling characters that advances a conflict and pushes the dramatic tension towards some sort of *resolution* and (gulp, I hate to use this word) catharsis, no? Isn't that what we expect of most of our theatre experiences? But does that necessarily mean it has to be naturalism or kitchen realism? It doesn't mean that in the long form, so why would it have to be so in the short? After all, Beckett was writing ten-minute plays before we had a new label for them. But what the new form does suggest is that there is little to no time to engage our audience with a dramatically compelling situation, so we have to fight the temptation to be clever or cute, and write idea plays that are thin on the "idea."

We'd all be wise to think this relatively new play-toy through, because the truth of the matter is that the ten-minute play isn't going to go away, slipping into obscurity like verse drama, because it falls out of fashion. As you read and as I write, it's digging in, pushing its paws into the dirt, wagging its tail in the face of purists and unwilling to budge because (1) writers perceive it's easy to write, (2) writers have a sense of completion and immediate gratification in a relatively short amount of time, (3) theatres, looking for forums to explore and expose a variety of new voices, are producing record numbers of festival of new ten-minute plays, (4) they're easy to produce, even by the poorest theatres and (5), audiences, our livelihood, are beginning to seriously appreciate ten-minute plays and look for their inclusion in a theatre season.

So now that we've thrashed about the good, the bad and the ugly of it all, let's figure out how to write something that'll make yo' mama shout "Howdy!"

I believe that as an actor, director or writer if you can speak truthfully for 10 minutes you can do it for 100. I have always been drawn to the 10-Minute play because in a single breath you can see deeply into the eyes of the playwright, the actors and the director and discover if there is a connection there between all of us.

~ Jeremy Skidmore,
Artistic Director of The Source
Theatre Festival in Washington, D.C.

CHAPTER 2

Work Those Ruby Slippers, Dorothy

Nobody likes to be told what to do, especially me. I'm a Taurus and I defy you to find someone more stubborn, opinionated and determined than me. Having grown up in the south, I was known as bull-headed; being educated in the north, I became known as a "pain in the butt" in class. Why? Because I've never wanted to think "in the box." I've always wanted to explore well beyond the box. To *insist* I go right just about guarantees I'll take a sharp left; *demand* I paint the sky blue and you'll see cherry red glowing from the heavens; *try to convince* me there's only one conceivable way to solve a problem and I'll work hard to give you ten solutions. If Glenda the Good Witch had said to me, "Follow the yellow brick road," I would have jumped in with "Why? What's up with the muddy stone path?" It's not that I intentionally want to be difficult, but it's been my experience that the unexpected, the less obvious or typical is far more interesting to me as a person and writer.

Thumbing my nose at rules and regulations has pushed me down some very interesting, exciting, but often troublesome paths; no more so than when I started to learn the craft of playwriting, 'cause there are plenty-o-rules to be broken there. But early on, after I had spun in circles for about five years (not attractive at any age), breaking every rule I could find and *getting no where*, I realized that I had a choice to make: learn and live by the rules or risk not finding an audience for what I wanted to say. I opted for the former because it was more important for me to find an audience than it was to placate the rebellious little boy in me. And to be really honest with you, part of that conversion was finally admitting to myself that I wasn't clever enough, or maybe even good enough, to defy convention and create my own aesthetic.

You do what you want to do, write what you want to write, 'cause I don't think anyone could convince you otherwise. Stand your ground! Be the writer you want to be. But if that stack of rejection letters gets larger than your desire to sit down and write another play, you might want to rethink your position. You can be the best quarterback in the world, but if you don't have a football team to play on, who's going to know? (I can't believe I used a sport analogy – I don't even like sports).

But if you are an advice-seeker looking for some direction when writing your ten-minute play that may, in some part, increase its chances for success (however you define that), here are some tools to help you do that. Tools are a means to a very particular end, so you gotta work those ruby slippers, Dorothy, if you wantta get home.

#1 Create Compelling Characters in Conflict

You will never find a story, plot, theatrical device, notion, idea or means of expression more interesting than the *people, or characters,* you create for your play. How could you, really? People are infinite in their complexity; stories are finite in their details. We're all passionate beings that are in a constant state of emotional highs and lows that demand action and reaction. And we're creatures of extremes: not only can we love a person for what we want, we can kill then for the same thing. We're fascinating beings that need to be understood through thoughts, reasoning, discussions, rationalizations, memories and negotiations – to name a very few.

A character created for the stage should reflect at least some small portion of our complexity as human beings. Part of that complexity, and an excellent place to begin the development of any character, is to identify what he/she *needs, wants, desires* in the situation you create for them. When we truly want something, it implies an action will follow, and plays, no matter what their length, are all about dramatic *action.* You're reading this book because your teacher is requiring you to and you *want* a good grade. Or you're reading this book because you *desire* to write a better ten-minute play, because you *need* to be recognized as a good writer, because you *want/desire/need* to derail your friends' and family's doubts that you have what it takes to be a successful writer. In short, you're reading this book because you want *something,* even if it's just to be mildly distracted for a while. You need, and therefore you take action – it's that simple.

The characters in your play should strongly desire something either from the situation they're in or from one another. It's dramatically strong if they *want* it, but even stronger if they really *need* it and *must have it* for their happiness or well-being: a young college man needs to finally free himself of the memories of childhood abuse when his mother pays him an unexpected visit; morbidly afraid of being alone, an untrusting, older woman needs to find new companionship after the death of her husband; a respected bible teacher desperately needs to defend his reputation when accused of sexual harassment. Put these three people/characters on stage in any environment or situation, and you already have the genesis of drama because either they will get what they want or not, and that in and of itself creates a dramatic tension that audiences will watch to see resolved.

The examples above are situational conflicts – because of a situation they find themselves in, the person/character is forced into taking some sort of action. We can see that every day on television between the hours of 11:00 am and 3:00 pm: daytime t.v.'s soap operas. In theatre, we want something deeper, more ponderous and we do that by extending the situational conflict (will he/she get what he/she needs) out to an even larger question: can we every really forget or escape our past? How far are we willing to go to not be alone? How tall are the walls we're building around today's teachers? Too tall?

These are pretty hefty questions that don't require a particular style, form or kind of theatre. They can be posed in a searing drama or an outrageous comedy, but when it's all said and done, and the lights are coming down on your play, you've left your audience with something more than "Will Herbert find true happiness with Lance or will he just leave their island of sin once and for all? Who cares about Herbert and Lance if they're not three-dimensional people that we can identify with (and with names like Herbert and Lance, they need all the attention we can shower on them)? We identify with characters/people by recognizing in them the same needs, questions and desires we have.

If you create a central character with a recognizable need or want that pushes them to take some sort of action, your next task is really easy: give *everybody* in the play something they want or need and will either get or not get by the play's end. If you do that, step back and watch the fireworks begin. If I write a play about an overly conscientious, uptight teacher who holds four students after school for detention, and I make that teacher someone that above all else needs to be respected, and I create two students who need to be the center of attention, one student who needs to challenge authority and one student who needs peace and quiet, the conditions for conflict are great. If I create a fifth character, a principal who needs to pompously exercise her power and authority, that drops in on the class to "observe" the teacher, the conflict (at least for the teacher) increases in a big way when the students misbehave.

You can see, then – just by giving characters very simple things that they want in relation to the other people – how conflict is born. Wouldn't it be more interesting to write the pizza delivery boy as someone who desperately wants to be liked by everyone instead of just the guy who hands over the double-cheese special? Even if he has two lines, he'll be infinitely more interesting. And if in addition to giving him a want or need, you give him some interesting *behaviors*, well, partners, you'll be cooking with gas!

People behave. That's what they do. You can be at a distance, not even know what someone's saying and understand some part of the conversation by watching their behavior. I was at the gym today, headphones on tight, listening to some thump, thump, thump music and watching the two people in front of me talk (go figure) as they were running at break-neck speed on their treadmills. Even though their bodies were doing the same mechanical thing, trust me, their emotional bodies and faces were not. One guy clearly thought he was running the New York Marathon, sprinting like he was running through the same field of clover that Julie Andrews sang "The Sound of Music" in. You could tell the other poor guy wanted to be that enthusiastic but just couldn't because, clearly, HE HATES THE GYM and his running shorts kept attacking him. I never heard a word these two guys said, but believe me, I knew a lot about them because I watched them behave.

As a playwright, how can you write characters for the theatre without attaching some sort of behavior to them – behavior that indicates character? As you're reading this you're probably playing with your hair, wiggling your knee, shaking your foot, petting your cat, watching that cute thing walk across the library atrium for the fifth time, eating french fries or sawing off a fingernail with a sharp bicuspid. But you are doing something. You're physically and emotionally multi-tasking as you're reading this book.

So why create a character that is only, quite literally, a mouth-piece for what you want them to say? Wouldn't it be more interesting to write a librarian that wraps rubber bands around her thumbs all morning, then unwraps them all afternoon as she flirts with the guy who shelves the books? A proud home-boy from da Bronx is a much more interesting person if he not only wants a date with the young woman on the stoop, but spits on her when he talks, habitually trips up the stoop and always sings a lot – off key. He wants what he wants – the attention of the young woman, but his behavior is working against him in every conceivable way. A cop is just a cop until he sings Broadway show tunes.

You're asking, "all of this in a ten-minute play?" To which I answer, "Yeah, baby, and and even more." Within the construction of a ten-minute play, a good deal of this character development has to happen within the first two pages or sooner. We have to know exactly what's at stake for the central character, i.e., what she wants/needs/desires and how she behaves, not only in life, but in this particular situation *quickly* because we want to initiate the obstacles that are going to get in her way and produce an emotional struggle for her to get what she wants. And we do this much sooner than later in our ten-minute plays because we want to engage our audience fast, unfold the story to keep their attention and come to some earned resolution that seems plausible and satisfying. It's hard – no doubt about it, but when it works …ahhh, it's magic, isn't it?

#2 Use A Structure

I don't have a preference for traditional or non-traditional structures in any play form. But this I do know: *there has to be some form of structure that serves the storytelling of the play in an intelligent, thought-provoking way and that compels the audience to continue watching your story* (I'd bold and underline that if my editors would let me get away with it). One of your challenges as a playwright is to figure out how best to tell your story, either through the traditional structure of a clearly defined beginning, middle and end, or a variation on that – end, beginning, middle and then back to end, or just middle and end, or even a more film-like approach of snippets of conversation that jump time, place, worlds – *whatever*. But you should make a decision of what will best serve the idea of the your play and write from the beginning with that in mind. Clear storytelling, with a structure that supports it, is as important as any character you'll create.

If you write non-linear, non-traditional structures, you know there's no sense for us to talk about what happens on page one, three or eight since you uniquely define it by its very creation. Let me warn you, though, that even for just ten minutes, an audience needs to have an emotional attachment to something – person, place or thing – and it's hard to get emotionally engaged in an intellectual, emotional or philosophical idea when the stimuli that are presented are too random or obtuse.

If you're someone who's most comfortable with the traditional three-part structure that has a clear beginning, middle and end, I suggest that the conflict of the play, or central dramatic question that will be answered in the course of the play (in *The Glass Menagerie*: will Tom escape the painful memories of his past? In *A Doll's House*, will Torvald discover Nora's secret?) be positioned somewhere around the first line of the play.

What?!

That's right. I'm suggesting that you start the play closer to its "middle" and *imply* the beginning of the story throughout the scenes that follow. In other words, let's get right to the action. Start the play with the circumstances already heightened. Let's throw the audience right smack-dab into the spin cycle. Think about it this way: let's say you were going to start a play with the scenario of a couple arguing about their relationship. He's not happy, she not's happy, she thinks he's cheating on her because he's grown cold, even aloof. He doesn't kiss her anymore, never touches her and hasn't said a romantic thing to her in years. She might even say something like, "If I didn't know better, I'd say you were trying to push me away – to get rid of me." Outraged, he leaves the apartment, slamming the door.

She crosses to the couch, furious, picks up the remote and surfs the televison channels. The door bell rings. She turns off the t.v., closes her robe with a tight twist of the belt, crosses to a mirror, checks her hair, crosses to the door, looks through the peep hole and says, "Who is it?" She hears somebody mumble something, decides it's safe and opens the door, steps back and gasps. You could do that (at least two pages worth of your script, minimum), but do we really need to see all of that stuff?

Why not this: lights up, the door's already open, the woman in the robe takes a step back, gasps and in walks a man holding a gun at face level. Wham! We jump right into the action. We don't know who, what or why, but you can bet we want to find out. Immediately we're drawn into questions of "What's going on? Who is he? Who is she? Do they know each other? What's with the gun?" And questions, cowboys and cowgirls, are good things in drama because they imply some sort of dramatic action and subtlety seduce an audience into emotionally investing in their answers.

In the example above, we can find out all of the information about her failing marriage (or the beginning of the play that we don't see) as the women in the robe suspects the guy with the gun was hired by her husband to kill her. It isn't until the guy with gun is in the apartment for five minutes (or, half-way through the play) that the woman in the robe realizes that he's at the *wrong* apartment: she's apartment 2A; he's looking for the person that lives in 2B.

Look, we only have ten minutes, so let's get it moving and shaking from the get-go. How bad could that be? But if you're not comfortable with this idea, and you need something a little more traditional (a true beginning, middle and end), then your conflict has to be articulated in a ten-minute play, I would think, no later than at the end of page two or the beginning of page three (the actual page numbers are suggestions; there's nothing that exact).

In those first two pages, show us the world we're in, set up your characters, reveal what's at stake for them and let us watch them behave in the world you've given them. At the end of those first couple of pages, make sure it's absolutely clear what the conflict is (from the previous example, will the woman in the robe get out of this alive?) If you follow traditional structure, you should be so clear about what the conflict is by page two that I could get up from my chair, leave the theatre and tell the first person I see: "It's the story of a group of good-hearted guys who may or may not lose their life savings in the stock market."

Moving forward, we go to pages three through eight or nine, and our goal is to complicate the story in such a way that the audience has no idea how the conclusion will turn out – keeping the dramatic suspense factor high. In the longer, more traditional forms, we might label this Act II, dramatically significant for its multiple complications and rising dramatic action/tension. In a ten-minute play, you have to find the right balance of story complications that can be resolved in the short span of the play. To do so, set your conflict in motion and then complicate the story by (1) introducing other characters who desperately need something themselves and can either help or hinder the central character; (2) introducing unforseen events that alter the course of the story; or (3) letting your central character have a change of heart/mind/soul/gender – anything that will *intensify* that central dramatic question that begs to be answered.

Obviously, you don't have a lot of time or play-space to outrageously complicate the story in five or six minutes. So my advice is to find one or two complications to the central story that catapult the conflict forward. For example, a young woman longs to regain a connection with her estranged family. When she wins the state lottery and becomes an instant millionaire, she's faced with a real dilemma: should she tell her perpetual-out-of-work, alcoholic father and petty criminal brother who both live in a neighboring town? Will they take advantage of her? Will they reappear in her life for all the wrong reasons? Complication #1: the media want her photograph for the area newspaper. Complication #2: her boyfriend, who never understood her family dynamic, chides her for being so selfish. Complication #3: unaware of her new wealth, the father shows up at her front door, unannounced and drunk.

The last page or so is all about resolution of the conflict and the restoration of a balanced world for the central character. Using the example above, the young woman's world was relatively balanced when the lights first rose on stage, then unbalanced quickly when she won the lotto. Her dramatic journey, of course, is to try to restore some sort of emotional balance to her world given the new complication in her life. The last page or so of that play should be about what the young woman will or will not do about sharing her good fortune with her family. Most dramatically pressing is her father, and whatever choice she'll ultimately make (to tell him or not) is directly affected by what she needs from him: his love; to be left alone; to be loved for what she is and not what she now has; to keep things simply at the status quo.

So to wrap it all up for you in a nice, neat package sans the red bow, if you're writing traditional structure for your ten-minute play, it would look something like this:

> Pages 1-2: set up the world we're in, introduce your central character(s), and make sure we understand what they need/want/desire in the journey of the story.
>
> Pages 2-3: illuminate the central conflict – a dramatic question that has an answer at the play's end.
>
> Pages 3-8: complicate the story-conflict two or three times.
>
> Pages 9-10: resolve the conflict, even if that creates an unhappy ending.

#3 Create Interesting Dialogue

I know, I know. Easier said than done, right? But in a ten-minute play, every theatrical element counts for something more than in a longer play, because we don't have the luxury of time to engage an audience. Every utterance has to count for something, and what better way to define character quickly than in sharp, revealing dialogue?

I don't know if you can truly teach someone to write dialogue, but I do know one thing that makes dialogue for the stage interesting and less ordinary. *No one speaks the same.* I know this may sound simple-minded, but the truth is we often write some sort of generic talk-language in our plays with nothing that has identifiers of character. We'd all be better dramatists if, once and for all, we acknowledge that *no two people speak the same because no two people are the same. How we speak, why we speak, is a fingerprint of our historical selves.*

We come from different states, countries, cultures, educational backgrounds, family dynamics, political interests, religions and on and on. Our speech is as unique to each of us as our finger prints, but for some reason we flatten people out when we put them on stage. If you're not sure what I'm talking about, do this simple experiment: take a page of any play of yours that has more than three characters. Using some sort of liquid paper/white-out, erase the names of your characters. Now make a xeroxed copy of your page, hand it to a friend and ask them to identify how many people are talking on the page. If you're like most of my students, you'll be shocked at the answers that come back to you. If you're really daring, try the same experiment with a page from a play that has five or six characters talking.

A person who is a thirty-five year old rigid academic isn't going to speak the same way a thirty-five year old brain surgeon with a highly developed IQ is going to speak, even if they've lived across the hall from each other all their lives. Yes, chances are they're both intelligent, well-read, career-minded people, but what makes them different in their use of language? Maybe the brain surgeon reads comic books in her spare time, watches *American Idol* every week, has never embraced the idea of a nutritional diet, knows the lyrics to every James Taylor tune he ever wrote and lives to party on the mountain slopes of Colorado. Maybe the rigid academic has a father who is a lawyer, a mother who is a psychiatrist, and for his personal enjoyment, devoutly reads *The Smithsonian* and *The Chronicle of Higher Education* and compulsively watches The Shopping Network. If we put these two people in the same room, *they're not going to sound the same.*

Your job as a playwright is to listen, remember, replicate and imitate how people talk. Some people talk with textbook English; others can barely string three words together in a simple statement. Some people talk in grand images and poetic metaphors; other talk with a saturation of four-letter words. Some people use forty words for one simple idea; others use two words for one complicated idea. Some people use words like "splendiferous;" others use "cool." Some folks use double-negatives ("It ain't no use in tellin' me that."); some use double-adjectives ("It was wicked cold"). If you're from New Orleans, you sound different than if you're from Boise. If you're shy, you speak one way, and if you're gregarious, another. And beyond the cultural or educational differences in people, if they're nervous, anxious, angry, tired, drunk, happy or sad, they'll sound even more different. That's what makes us special, individual, unique. So make your characters special, make them different. In a ten-minute play, a writer can tell me loads about a person by the way he speaks, leaving more stage time to develop the story and plot points.

#4 Use Your Sense of the Theatrical

That, of course, assumes that you have a sense of the theatrical. If you don't, think about this: what makes theatre, theatre? What can you do in theatre that you can't do on television or film? What do live actors bring to the occasion? An audience? A director's vision? If we see an actor literally fly across the stage, why is it more special in a theatre than if we see an actor in a film do the same thing? Keep asking yourself: what makes theatre, theatre? Those Greeks used a chorus for something; Brecht got in your face for some reason; Chekhov made you wait endlessly for some purpose. And it all has to do with that which is inherently theatrical – that which requires a live audience to experience the thrill of live performance guided by your thoughts as a writer, your ideas and your sense of creating worlds that we ordinarily don't see – or at least see from your perspective.

Break out of the box and consider setting your play on the wing of an airplane (if it's appropriate). Have a modern-day chorus of three cab drivers report Rachel's journey to the Big Apple. Have your characters engage the audience, pitch a ball to the audience – for that fact, serve burgers to the audience if it makes sense to the storytelling of your play. Underscore that serious confrontation scene between mother and daughter with an inexplicable baby's cry in the distance. Intensify the light so bright that it's blinding when the building contractor finally comes clean with his dirty business deals. Flood the stage with exaggerated sounds of a business office over the wedding scene or the sound of a clock incessantly ticking if it serves the idea you're exploring.

Open your imagination to what the theatre can provide. Remember, we can isolate and amplify light, sound and people. We can tell an audience where to look and control how long they hold their gaze. We can paint the world solid blue with one red dot hanging mysteriously in the air. Or, we can create a realistic booth in a diner that's as interesting as any of the above. As my colleague Michael Wright has said many times before in his books on playwriting, "remember, playwriting is Play At Writing."

#5 Be Specific

There is nothing more glorious to an audience than to be seduced by specific, imagistic writing. If you're telling an old friend about the house you grew up in, obviously the more specific you are about the color of the house, the expanse of the front yard, the crooked, cracked driveway and the tree you climbed in on summer nights, the better chance he has of appreciating your emotional recollection and memory. If as a playwright, you want me to understand that one of your characters has just completed a road trip across the country, then you can add to my enjoyment of the tale if your character tells me the trip was made in a Aqua Blue '67 Thunderbird Convertible that he bought from a retired World War II veteran who cried the day he sold it.

Your character can tell me the road trip was "great fun," or he can tell me "the only time I remember having that much fun was when my dad and I got lost in Yosemite National Park for three days with two Japanese tourists who knew four words in English: Hello, good-bye and bathroom, please." He can tell me "the car drove great," or he can say, "the car glided down the highway like it was skating on ice." The more specific you are in your writing, the larger the world you create for me. Without knowing it, I'm in your world, fully participating in my imagination, and all you did was draw me in with the help a few specific words. And if I'm going to be in your world for such a short time, let me see it from every angle you can think of.

#6 Worry About What's Too Much

An explanation by way of a painful example: I was working somewhere away from New York and was invited to a showcase of ten-minute plays centered around the theme, "What Would You Say If You Finally Had the Chance to Say It?" Oy vey. Before I ever got there I knew I was in big trouble.

What appeared on stage was a series of ten-minute plays in which the central character finally got to say to whomever what they'd always wanted to say about some past injury, insult, disappointment or heartache. And because the writers were for the most part inexperienced (at least I hope that was the excuse), what we were treated to was two hours of people ranting about everything – and I do mean *everything* – that ever made them angry about the other person. Each play started with the central character just addressing one issue connected to the other person, but inevitably soon grew to an out and out indictment of every ill of their relationship. It was exhausting, frustrating…and uninteresting. Why?

First, the theme, which of course appeared in print, tipped off the audience to the central dramatic action. We knew there was going to be a car wreck and we were just waiting to see when it was going to happen and if somebody was going to lose a head or an arm. Secondly, and most important, almost all of the writers saturated the ten minutes with so many issues between the two people that it left me to wonder, how are they going to resolve all of that in such a short amount of time? Silly me. What was I thinking? There was no resolution – just a hefty ol' dose of "Good! I feel better now that I've gotten that off my chest." Finally, and don't ask me why or how this happened, almost all of the secondary characters never got a chance for a rebuttal. They had to just sit there and take it! Later I thought, well, that was actually a good thing because if they had started in with *their* issues about the other person, my head would have exploded.

The scope of what you write has to fit inside that very small ten-minute container. Granted, there has to be conflict that is resolved to some sort of audience satisfaction. But if you top-load the play with too many character issues (her brother hates her; her sister steals from her; the landlord's threatening to sue her for her back rent and she didn't get accepted to the college of her choice), either you're writing a farce (where compound issues are essential), or teetering on melodrama. If you're writing about a relationship that's ending between two people, let it be ending because of one or two painful, irreconcilable differences between the two, not twenty.

"But I know people like that. I know relationships that have that many problems," I can hear some of you saying. Fine. Get them all to a therapist. But don't put them on stage as characters unless you're making a very intelligent, very purposeful comment about their life situation. An audience that has too much to care about (or invest in) often ends up caring about nothing because it's simply too overwhelming in such a short amount of time.

#7 Avoid the Park Bench Play

Question (or a joke, depending on your perspective): how many short plays ever written have been set in a park on a bench? Answer: too many. Too effin' many. So many that if I never saw another, I'd be a happier man. And for some reason, a short play seems to beg writers to be set on a park bench. There are so many more interesting places that two people can happen on one another: a baseball game, divorce court, at confession, at a bar mitzvah, at an art auction or funeral, tennis game, pig wrestling competition – just about anywhere you can imagine. Ahhhhhhh, there's the AOL key word: Imagine. Use your imagination and get off the park bench unless you really need a park to serve the play.

#8 The F-Word

Okay, relax. I'm not going to say don't use it. I'm not even going to suggest how often you use it. I will say this: if you didn't use the f-word, what would be in its place? Just think about it sometime. Yeah, I know: people talk like that. A lot of people talk like that. I talk like that. But when I do, it's because other people around me are talking like that, or they expect me to talk like that, or I'm trying to fit in, or stand out, or sound hip, or sound younger than I am. As a writer, wouldn't it be more dramatically interesting if you could find a good behavioral reason to use the f-word instead of using it as phonetic comma?

#9 Play the Format Game

Absolutely, undeniably, without a shadow of a doubt, make a cover page for your play with the title, your name and contact information including all phone numbers and email addresses. A second page should follow that is devoted to a character breakdown, listing each character's name, sex, age and any physical, emotional or relationship information we need to know to start the play (Naomi, F., 25: tall, brittle, angry; mother of twins). Also on this page, you can provide for us the time and location of the story: "New York City, Upper West Side tenement building, 1972." These two pages DO NOT count in the overall page numbers of your play, so don't sweat it and do do it. Number the first page of dialogue as Page 1. When you don't do this, and you put all of that contact and character information on your first page of dialogue, you're eating up valuable space. And there are a lot of theatres that systematically don't read plays that go beyond that tenth page in number.

#10 Know That You Don't Have to Agree with or Completely Understand #1-9 and You Can Still Write a Good Play

Look, all of this information comes from my experiences of writing and teaching for a lot of years. I take this stuff from the mistakes I've made, mistakes I've seen other people make and from watching how other writers succeed in the theatre. I've tried to share with you what I've experienced as valuable lessons I've learned the hard way, but it may not hit you in any kind of meaningful way. So take what I've suggested that resonates for you, let it work its way into your creative psyche and then write your ten-minute play the way you want to write it. If you find you're not making the mark in your own definition of success, re-read #1-9 and see if it makes any more sense to you. If it does, good. If it doesn't, keep writing. You'll figure it out.

And if all else fails, read the next chapter: how to figure out if you're sabotaging your own writing.

You've got rules and regulations, yes, but through this confinement, you've got the chance for this EXPLOSION of creativity. With limitations, there is immense creative freedom. A whole world of creativity is going to open up when you set the story of your play in a cardboard box. When you put the world of your play in the middle of Grand Central Station, it's less interesting.

~ Laura Margolis, Producing Manager
StageWorks, Hudson, New York

Chapter 3

My Ten-Minute Play Sucks. What The F?

Sometimes writers (myself included) are just big, fat, sloppy, snotty-nosed, sticky-fingered babies. We don't want someone to tell us what to do! We don't want someone telling us how to create our art! We don't want someone to put us in a playpen and say, "you can only play in here – in this square. Not out there. Not over there. In here. Just here." But when we're writing ten-minute plays, let's acknowledge one simple fact: a human being – usually a harried producer – actually has to *produce* the play you've written. Hello? Slap yourself in the face and wake up for this. SOMEONE HAS TO ACTUALLY *PRODUCE* THE PLAY YOU'VE WRITTEN. And regardless of any argument you or I can make about artistic freedom or artistic expression, someone has to translate your written word to a visual representation on stage. So be smart, and avoid that "My play sucks. And it feels like nobody loves me. Why?" conversation you've had with every friend that would listen.

When a producer is organizing an evening of ten-minute plays, he has to consider the available resources (money, directors, actors, rehearsal time, tech time, technical limitations, publicity) in relation to the number of playwrights being produced. On the most basic level, eight playwrights equals eight plays, equals eight mini-productions. Therefore, it only makes sense that we make our plays not only dramatically attractive, but also production-wise. If we construct our play in such a way that it means one less production headache for the producer, our chances of getting produced aren't guaranteed, but they're better than at least fifty percent of the others. Consider a recent experience I had:

I was producing a ten-minute play festival for an Off-Off-Broadway theatre in New York that had no wing space, no fly space, a small room backstage that could fit five, maybe six sets of the Olsen Twins shoulder to shoulder and a few technical necessities – your typical under-funded, over-stressed New York black box. A young woman submitted a play that I thought was absolutely brilliant – a word I rarely, if ever, use to describe someone's writing. There was only one small problem: the text called for a flying bicycle. That's right. A bicycle that magically flew across the space, back and forth, up and down. You couldn't do the play without the image of the flying bicycle, so of course, I couldn't produce the play and it broke my heart. I called the writer to tell her how much I liked the play but couldn't produce the piece because of the inherent technical problem in the text. She said, "Gosh, I never thought about that."

Think about it. I'm begging you. I'm pleading with you. Don't break my heart because I love your play but can't possibly produce it. Here are ten things to my mind that you can leave out of your work when you write. And if you do, maybe we'll meet each other one day when I call to say, "Congratulations, we'd like to produce your play."

#1 Insane Settings - The Producer's Point of View

Don't set your play in the kitchen of a four-star restaurant that requires three ovens, two stoves, five waiters, and two dueling chefs preparing a full dinner for the President of the United States. Remember, there's a producer behind this production, and s/he's counting bucks, people power, favors owed and hours in the day to produce not just your play but six or seven others. It takes money to have all that stuff. It takes technicians to drag it on and off the stage. It takes *time* to drag it on and off the stage – more time that an evening of ten-minute plays can afford.

I know you think a dorm room's just a dorm room – nothing fancy there. But if you're writing realism, then that dorm room has to have beds, a table, chairs, books, computers, posters and vomit stains on the carpet from that miserable frat boy who blew chunks in the room on a drunken Saturday night. So be smart. Note in the text, "a dorm room represented by a table, chair, computer and a 'Go Cardinals!' poster for the Lamar University football team." Let someone know that you've thought of an easy way to establish the setting of your play that won't give the designers a nervous breakdown.

#2 Insane Settings - The Designer's Point of View

Don't set your play on the front porch of a two-story, restored Victorian house that we're supposed to see both inside and upstairs. Remember, there's a production stage manager and set designer behind this production (not to mention a limited budget), and s/he's got to design a space that eight different plays can work in and can be moved into and out of with ease and speed. Your play is not stand-alone; it has to fit within the context of an evening of plays.

I know I told you to think "out of the box," and I still want you to do that. But be reasonable in your thinking. Here's my own personal, secret formula. Before I set my ten-minute plays anywhere I say to myself: "If I had to build the set of my play all by my lonesome self, where would I set the play?" Chances are you may find yourself in just that position. I know I have. And you really don't want me anywhere near a hammer and nails and certainly no power tools. So the simpler the better. Everyone will thank you.

#3 Insane Casting

Don't have a Dancing Sailor Chorus of fifteen: make it three, tops, if that many. If you do that, you've got those three, the Captain, the Captain's girlfriend, the Captain's girlfriend's boyfriend, his lover, his lover's father, and his lover's father's parrot (I know it can be the Stage Manager dressed in green garbage bags and a smart yellow cap, but he still has to be counted). Okay, that's a total of nine people in ten pages. Wheeeewwwwww! That's a lot of folks in a little time. And can you really get an actor to do the part of the Captain when all he does is limp on stage with an oak-branch-as-cane, look at the Dancing Sailor Chorus and say, "Velveeta, anyone?" It's not impossible, but I think it'd be a hard sell to a producer that you actually need nine people for your short ten-minute play, especially since one of those characters has only one line. Also, and I know this shouldn't be a real consideration, trying to juggle the lives of nine actors, one director, one writer, one stage manager and other technicians can be a nightmare. You might as well be doing *Angels in America, Parts I & II*, for all of that effort.

#4–5 Insane Technical Requirements

Don't have thirty sound cues (#4), or fifty-two light cues (#5), or eight changes of costume (#5A) unless you want to see a very haggard and intensely cranky technical crew. Remember, there are technicians behind this production that have to punch the buttons, pull the levers, time the fade-outs, score the music up, shoot the gun off , pull the shoes off while putting the shirt on and strike the tin-sheet for the thunder effect. And aesthetically, if you overburden your ten-minute play with technical requirements, it could look and sound more like a video clip from the People's Choice Awards than a play.

Since your work is not a stand-alone play, the lighting designer has to use all lighting instruments for all plays. Maybe s/he can give you one isolated spotlight center stage; but I guarantee you s/he can't give you eight isolated spots. The costume designer has to work with a number of casts and costume requirements, usually begging, borrowing or stealing where s/he can to costume actors. A sound designer (if you're that fortunate) has to make, cue, re-cue and instruct the board operator for every sound cue in the whole evening, not just your play.

Now, having said all of that, don't be afraid to fill the world of your play with what you feel is thematically or dramatically necessary. But do consider every technical requirement as one small piece of a much, much larger pie.

#6 The Writer You Want to Murder

Don't think that the label "ten-minute play" couldn't possibly apply to your fifteen minutes of work. Wouldn't it be a drag to get a call from an artistic director who says they'd love to do your play if you'll considering cutting five minutes out of it? In the longer form, that's the equivalent of cutting Act One from a three-act play. Playwrights for some reason haven't grasped the concept that ten minutes *means* ten minutes, not twelve and certainly not fifteen. All those "it's only eleven/twelve/thirteen minutes" arguments are a real crock. Consider this: if a producer's got your play, and if it's fifteen minutes, and s/he's got seven other plays that clock in at fifteen minutes, you're looking at an evening of ten-minute plays that should be seventy minutes plus intermission, but is in reality, one hundred and five minutes plus intermission. Add in scene changes, and it's beginning to look like a very long evening of theatre.

Here's another problem with cheating the time/minute thing: audiences know that what they're supposed to be watching is a ten-minute play. When a play starts to clock in around twelve or thirteen minutes, the audience (myself included) starts thinking, "this isn't ten minutes. This isn't even twelve minutes." But even more important than that, they've stopped paying attention to your play.

Playwrights are stubborn. They don't want to accept the limitation of the form and instead try to find ways to trick the producer's eye (smaller fonts, larger margins). We're not that blind, ya'll. We see what you're doing. And even if your play has the magical number of "ten" on the last page, don't think this means (because we don't) that it's ten minutes long. So do the hard-boiled egg thing and TIME IT! That's right. Sit down, read it out loud, and time the thing. That way you're sure, and you'll never get that "cut it" phone call.

#7–9 Three Ways to Cheat the System That Don't Work And Make You Look Bad

When I see the following on the physical page in a ten-minute play, I know exactly the kind of writer I'm dealing with. Don't do this to yourself; don't do it to me. I want to like you, not ignore you. When you change the font on your typeface (bad move #7) so you can cram fourteen pages into ten, I can see that like the flashing neon sign it is. Your script should be written in a twelve-point font. When you expand the margins from the usual one-inch parameter towards the edges of the page (bad move #8) to a half-inch to fit more script in, I can see this like a billboard in my front yard. When you shrink the spacing between character names, dialogue and stage directions (bad move #9) to fit more script in, I can see that like a car driving through my kitchen window. It's that obvious.

#10 The Dangling Third

It's your call, but when you write ten pages and a third, there are some theatres that will throw your script in the trash. To many producing organizations, the only way they can assure some consistency in the time factor (though I'm not really convinced it works) is to make a hard and fast rule that if it's longer than ten pages, it can't be considered for production. You may see this as silly, but they see it as practical. So, yeah, I know: it's just five lines on page eleven, but for some producers, that's five lines too many.

I've been there. I know what it's like to not want to cut those five lines just to get it to page ten. So do this: look through the script and see if there are any stage directions or parenthetical actor directions that can be eliminated. Is there any dialogue that is repetitive? Is there a whole dramatic beat that can be shortened or cut altogether? Can you combine sections of dialogue by one character and streamline what they say? Give it a shot; see what happens.

❦ ❦ ❦

Look, I'm for anything that gets writers writing and theatres being exposed to more voices. But a ten-minute play will go where? Most likely in a ten-minute play festival for the Theatre Behind The Bowling Alley because (1) they're relatively easy to produce, (2) audiences are treated to a diversity of voices, (3) they're great opportunities for actors, (4) they're a terrific challenge for designers, and (5) theatres are introduced to a number of new playwrights they can nurture and cultivate relationships with.

At NYU, I produced our annual Ten-Minute Play Festival for ten years and here's what I had to play with: a rectangular stage area twenty-five feet wide by seventeen feet deep, a.k.a., "tiny"; a ceiling twelve feet high with a light grid that could barely keep the lighting instruments off the heads of the audience; barely four feet of backstage area; no wings, no sides, no teasers, no curtains; no green room for the actors; a regulation door that functioned as an emergency exit at the lip of the stage, and no costume or prop storage. All of those conditions had a *profound* effect on what I could reasonably produce in that space. I didn't want to make myself or my actors, directors and technicians miserable, and perhaps most importantly, disappoint a writer because I couldn't serve the vision of his/her play. And just so you know, that NYU theatre is not unlike a good number of the smaller theatres in this country. My situation there of fitting the play to the space is hardly uncommon.

So, if you're going to write in this genre, write so you'll be produced. Otherwise, what's the point?

Sometimes the set is just a door...I'm one to keep it as simple as possible.

~ B. J. Scott, Artistic Director
Camino Real Playhouse

CHAPTER 4

Serious Murder on Your Mind:

Problems in Production and the People Who Cause Them

If you're a writer, DON'T TURN THE PAGE because you think this doesn't apply to you. Everything about your art, including its production, applies to you. So hunker down, read on and appreciate what has to happen to create even the smallest world for a ten-minute play. If you're an artistic director, producer or stage manager, read this as the gospel it is, 'cause, ooooooh, mercy, I've had to learn the hard way.

I produced my first ten-minute play festival ten years ago (and lived to tell the story). Even though I'd produced a hundred or so one-act and full-length plays, never, *never* could I predict the quicksand-as-art that I experienced. Never mind that I am compulsively organized; forget that I have lots more resources than most small theatres; fuhgettabout the small army that I always have working with me – because nothing could have prepared me for what was ahead. Okay, I admit: part of the problem was my own blind ignorance, but a good part of the problem is the nature of the beast – there's just too much going on in a very small amount of time with tons of people everywhere. What's more, producing a group of ten-minute plays, year to year, is production-unique because each year there's a different kind of struggle with each new group of playwrights, plays, directors and actors. So sit back and learn from somewhere who's been there, done that, sold the leftover t-shirts on the street corner.

#1 Forcing a Size 12 Foot into a Size 4 Shoe

Let's say, for the sake of discussion, you're producing eight ten-minute plays for one evening's worth of theatre and that you're going to run that evening four days a week for three weeks (a standard Equity showcase code contract). No matter how you slice it, Chef, you're producing eight different plays with eight different casts and directors. And even though they're each ten minutes, they might as well each be a full-length play for all the work that you're going to put into them.

What will make you or break you is technical support staff. You *NEED* an efficient, hard-working staff that can accommodate the sheer volume of people (and egos) involved. When I produced our annual festival at NYU, that translated to eight directors, one set designer, one lighting designer, one costumer designer, one production stage manager (PSM), two assistant stage managers (ASMs) and a cracker-jack running crew (lights, sound and backstage) of at least three or four people. I can almost hear you gulp: I'm not suggesting that you have to have all of these folks in place. There are some people, however, that are just plain indispensable.

You can never have too many hands in a production like this, and you need one lone person who's in charge of them all. You *NEED* a PSM beyond the individual stage manager(s) for any one play. Why? Traffic. Lots of it. Loads o' people – everywhere. You need one responsible, attempting-to-be-calm person in charge who's not trapped for hours at any one play's rehearsal – someone at home base who can see and understand the BIG picture and organize it.

S/he will schedule all of your production meetings, follow up on that endless list of production details that grows larger as time passes, serve as the liaison between the designers and the directors, coordinate rehearsal schedules and dress rehearsals – in effect, function as the director of the evening. More importantly, this person schedules and executes that maddening technical weekend/week prior to opening, wherein eight different casts with a pile of directors descends on the theatre to set technical cues. Someone has to stay on the clock to keep everyone sane and focused; a competent PSM can do that and more.

My two ASMs were assigned four plays each. They attended rehearsals, recorded blocking, kept the production book, shopped for simple stage props, took notes – all the standard responsibilities of a stage manager, and reported weekly to the PSM. You'll find the single biggest problem the ASMs have to work through, whether they're covering two plays or five, is having to be in different places often at the same time because of the different rehearsal schedules. At NYU, it would have been nice if I had had eight different stage managers (one for each play), but I didn't and never would because I can barely afford the two. So it requires that everyone coordinate their efforts (primarily directors) to accommodate the ASMs. The only other solution is to do away with the ASMs altogether and have the director serve some of the basic stage manager functions – not the ideal situation, but workable.

In production, the ASMs are in the light and sound booth calling the show, usually alternating their effort every other play (it keeps them fresh and alert). In situations where I don't have ASMs, my PSM attends enough rehearsals to understand the flow of each play then brings the show into tech-weekend and calls each show from the booth. It can work, but it can also age the PSM years ahead of his/her time because they are responsible for everything from the time an actor shows up at the theatre to that final light cue at the end of the evening. And of course, whatever s/he does for one play, s/he does for eight.

Your running crews (the most under-appreciated people in the theatre) have to be some of the most dedicated, committed and diligent workers you can find. Whatever you do, don't give this area of the production over to the slackers hanging around your theatre. I've made this mistake, thinking, "how bad could it be?" Trust me: it's a nightmare because these folks have to change sets, set props, re-patch dimmers, quick-change an actor and cue the stage manager in less than a minute. Multiply all of this by eight in one evening just for each play's *pre-show*, let alone what happens in the interior and at the conclusion of each play, and you can appreciate the job that's in front of them. You need a group of team players who operate together like a finely-oiled piece of machinery, and aren't eating Captain Crunch out of the box while listening to techno-house music on their IPod.

I know this sounds like an awful lot of people working on what should be a relatively simple production, and you're right, it is. But don't try to put a size twelve foot in a size four shoe. Better over-staffed than under, particularly if it's your first time doing it. If you've got favors due you in the community, put the call out. In this kind of production, you won't be sorry to see so many people working together towards the common good. You'll be left to produce and promote the show with a clear, thinking head, and you might have only five sleepless nights instead of fifteen.

#2 Bottle-Necking: Fifty Actors or Five

If you're doing eight plays, you can count on casting at least sixteen actors (two actors for each play), minimum. When some plays require three, four or five characters, your casting needs multiply. There are two ways to approach casting, and your choice ultimately rests with how you need to serve the artists connected to your company. If you have ten or so actors that make up the core of your acting company, you can cast actors in multiple roles from different plays. This can be a good thing for several reasons: (1) actors are challenged trying to define a variety of character-types; (2) actors get to showcase their wide range of skill; (3) there are fewer people for your PSM to keep track of; (4) if you have limited dressing room space or backstage space, there are fewer people to juggle and fewer incidents of elbows-to-eyeballs; and (5) an audience gets a genuine kick out of seeing one actor transform for several different, often difficult roles.

But there are some down sides to multiple casting that will give you (or someone) a big ol' headache if you're not careful. There are eight plays that require eight different rehearsal schedules. You can't fault a director for believing his/her rehearsal is the most important, and understandably they want all of their actors at their rehearsals at all times. When you cast an actor in three or four different plays, there's got to be a lot of pre-planning or you'll have a lot of angry people on your hands, if you can't assure everyone of some quality time with each other.

Also, actors who attend a lot of different rehearsals are stretching their valuable time to begin with; rehearsals, coupled with working, studying for school, relationships, etc., leaves very little room for anything else. Actors need free head-time to work on their characters – something I know I've been guilty of forgetting in the past. They need preparation time; heck, they need some just good ol' down time. (If we treat them like cattle, they'll behave like cattle.) And finally, you should at least consider that an actor cast in three or four roles has to labor through hours and hours of technical rehearsals, eating up their energy at a time they need it the most. And just remember: when any one of us gets overly tired, that's when we stop doing our jobs well; in the theatre, that's when those ugly diva alter-egos rear their ugly heads.

If you have a large number of actors you want to serve, or if you just want to get to know a large pool of actors in a relatively safe venture, casting single actors for single roles in a festival of ten-minute plays is an ideal situation. Everyone wins: your directors will thank you because they don't have to negotiate rehearsal schedules among each other; you get to see a wide spectrum of talent for your future productions; your audience numbers increase because each actor invites a group of friends; and there's more people to help build the set, strike the set, scout for props and promote the evening.

The down side to single-role casting is obvious – bottle-necking everywhere. Do you have enough dressing room space? Green room space? Backstage space? Where do you put twenty-four actors? How can you accommodate their needs *prior* to a performance (physical and vocal warm-ups)? How do you accommodate their needs *during* performance? Do they take their curtain call after their individual performance and then leave the theatre, or do you draw everyone involved together at the end of Act One for their bows, then Act Two? Or do you have a full company bow at the end of Act Two? And if you do that, are you prepared for twenty-five actors to hang out for two hours until the curtain call? Do you limit everyone's playbill biographies to fifty words so that the program doesn't look like a phone book?

These are all very real, practical considerations that with some pre-planning and thought shouldn't be an issue. But you do have to think about them, and better sooner than later.

#3 Eight Can Feel Like Eighty

Do eight plays mean eight directors? Your call. Economics, people resources and time to find, hire and orient them to your theatre are certainly a consideration. It's eight additional people to deal with, and with so many people already involved, eight more people can feel like eighty. Regardless of how you configure the director thing, keep this in mind: the more directors you have, the more effort there will be to schedule rehearsals that don't conflict in the limited rehearsal space you have. There will be much more negotiating and compromising between your designers and directors to accommodate eight unique visions of the individual plays. And on a purely administrative level, it's more difficult to work around eight people's personal lives to schedule a production meeting than it is with four. Still, it's a great venue to see the work of eight different directors whom you're considering for larger, longer work in your theatre.

#4 Designer Mayhem

The scenic and lighting designers will have murder and mayhem on their minds if you don't allow them to conceptualize the evening of work using a unit set and repertory light plot. Trying to accommodate eight locations for eight very different plays interpreted through the eyes of different directors becomes a logistical nightmare. The design challenge is to integrate the individuality of each play into the working whole, and it's been my experience that the designers welcome that challenge over the alternative of trying to create eight unique environments.

If you incorporate the idea of a unit set – one environment that all plays must function in – the scenic designer's job is to make the look of the space interesting and suitable for all eight plays and functional for their action. It seems the most successful scenic designs I've seen are those that are not specific to any kind of realistic interior or exterior but are instead more of an open space in which the parameters are defined by the strategic placement of platforms, flats and some furniture. I don't know enough about design to suggest anything more concrete, but I do know that a booth at a diner, the front row of a movie theatre, the bow of a boat, the front seat of a car, a rocky crag in Scotland and an attendant's desk at a funeral home are all very real possibilities in the world of these plays. Simple, identifying set pieces that move in and out of the stage space freely and, most importantly, quickly, are often all you need to distinguish the location.

I've seen a harried producer/artistic director (and admittedly done this myself) face a group of directors and writers and say, "Look, you have four chairs, two tables, a park bench, two platforms and a bookshelf to make this work." It's not the ideal situation, (what if the play is set on a sandy beach?) but often times, that's truly all you have because of a limited budgets and personnel. Use what you have, but find someone with a creative eye to take those four chairs, two tables, a park bench, the platforms and the bookshelf and apply a unifying paint treatment or texture to them as well as the floors and walls. You want to try to avoid that "we just pulled this out of our garage" look because most audiences want a heightened theatrical atmosphere and not something that looks like what they park their Volvo next to every night. Like I said to the playwrights, limitations should force you to be more creative, not less.

What a scenic designer can't completely provide in terms of the individuality of each play, a lighting designer can. Every theatre has its own technical limitations, but if it's possible, allow your lighting designer to provide each play its own look, its own visual environment that will support the world of the play. You only may have twenty feet by twenty feet of actual performance space, but with a very creative lighting designer, that space can be made to look like twenty different places – just what you need when you're changing locales so often and quickly. If your resources are limited (and whose aren't, really), a standard repertory light plot plus a few strategically placed light-specials can provide enough of a difference to trick the eye into believing there's been a change in locations.

Your biggest headache when creating the performance environment is a people/artistic problem. What works aesthetically for one director or one writer will often not work for another. One director will tell you that the wide, open space your designer has created is perfect for his/her rocky crag in Scotland; another director will tell you that the space is too open to create the intimacy needed for the bedroom play. If you're dealing with talented designers, these problems can be solved easy enough. But many of us don't always have the luxury of true designers with well-stocked resources. My suggestion then falls to the writer: make sure we understand where we are in your play by what you say in your play – the audience will fill in the gap. They're cooperative that way.

#5 The Time Nazi

None of us has enough time – ever. It's never our friend. If I could balance my laptop in one hand while I'm writing this and stir a pot of chili for supper with the other, I'd do it, because I've never had enough time to do it all. And when you're producing a ten-minute play festival, time is the Big Enemy that everyone – in their zealousness to create – forgets. The writers are convinced that their plays are ten minutes long, regardless of the fact that they're clocking in at thirteen, fourteen and sixteen minutes. That's when you begin hearing, "if Brandon would only pick up his pace in scene one, the play would come in right on time," (Hello? Three minutes worth?) And because of these writers' short-sightedness, what the producer thinks is going to be an evening of ninety minutes will undoubtedly stretch to two hours. In performance, your audience is then aware of the time because they thought they were only coming to see eight ten-minute plays and they've done the simple math.

Directors get caught up in their rehearsal and forget that there is another director and cast waiting outside the rehearsal hall waiting to start their rehearsal. The director outside is steaming because s/he knows s/he's only got two hours before s/he loses her principle actor to another rehearsal. When the door opens between the two directors, they grumble and shoot each other nasty eye-daggers.

Tech days are a nightmare because the producer insists (in order to keep everyone sane) that each play gets only three hours of total tech time

– a total of twenty-four straight working hours for the technicians. The technicians think it's too much; the directors, not enough. Publicity people get frazzled because there are twenty-nine people in the company and only half have turned in their program biographies on time. The sound guy can't figure out for the life of him why one of the ten-minute plays has twenty-six sound cues and is frantically scurrying to get them all recorded and cued. At the end of the day, no one is satisfied; everyone goes home cranky. What to do?

Nothing. There's nothing you can do, except make everyone aware of how crucial it is that all involved respect time from every angle and to treat it like the elusive burglar it is. To that end, one of the smartest lessons I've learned over the years was to hold an all-company meeting before anyone goes into rehearsal. Invited is every human being working on the project. We sit, discuss and outline the effort at hand. That's when I introduce myself as the Time Nazi, and warn everyone – writers, directors, designers – about staying on the clock. Then I can be a hard-nosed when need be, because I've warned them. If I need the plays (for example) to come in on the ten-minute mark, and I've told the writer *early on*, "cut it or we'll drop it," then I can do just that and walk away with a clear conscience.

#6 The Playbill As Phone Book

When it comes to programs and publicity for your ten-minute plays, there can be names and biographies for days. Publicity postcards can look like a page out of your local phone book if you try to list everyone involved. The program can be practically unreadable because you've shrunk the font so small to fit in everyone's biography. What I've done in the past to solve the problem is workable: in the program and on the postcard/poster, only the writers, directors and designers are listed. Inside the program, the tech staff (including designers), directors and writers have biographies. On a wall outside the theatre, we post all of the actors' photographs (sometimes more than forty) with a handsomely typed biography posted in a readable font just below the photograph. The audience then has something to look at during the pre-show and intermission. If your actors don't have headshots, grab a disposable camera and have some fun.

#7 Hello? Is Anybody Out There?
The Disappearing Audience

I've tried everything I can think of to solve this problem, but people are people and whether we like it or not, a lot of the audience members are there only to see their friends. Once they see them, they leave and often don't wait until an intermission. This make me really crazy when I turn people away at the door who genuinely want to see the whole evening. And even though those that leave have paid full price for a ticket, they're still leaving the theatre half-empty for a group of actors to play to. Too many times I've seen the theatre jammed to the walls for Act I, and at the intermission, the audience empties out leaving four people to see Act II. But what can you do?

Two things: at the beginning of the show we make an announcement that it's unsafe for the audience to leave their seats in the dark during the show (true) and ask that they make every effort to wait until intermission. We also tell our actors that appear in Act II to tell their friends that if they can't secure a ticket for the top of the show, to come back to the theatre on the intermission and we'll let them in for half-price. Neither of these things solves the problem entirely, but it does cut down on some of the traffic in and out of the theatre and provides some sort of audience for Act II.

#8 Long Play's Journey Into Night

I included ten plays in the first festival of ten-minute plays I produced, thinking that it sounded cool to promote "Ten by Ten." The evening started at 8:05 and concluded at 10:40 pm.

No one was more surprised than me – unhappily so, I might add.

Everyone is fooled by the label "ten-minute play." It sounds short, and in fact, it should be short. But even if you have eight ten-minute plays that clock in right on time, that's eighty minutes. Add a minute change-over between plays (and even that's too long), and you're at eighty-eight minutes. Add a ten-minute intermission and now you're at ninety-eight minutes. Add five more minutes when you hold at the top of the show for late arrivals: a hundred and three minutes. Add five more minutes because not everyone could cycle through the bathrooms at intermission: a hundred and eight minutes. Now add two more plays because you think "they're only ten minutes": a hundred and twenty-eight minutes. Now add five more minutes for the unforeseen: a hundred and thirty-three minutes, or, two hours and thirteen minutes. Now you're producing something that's beginning to feel like *Long Day's Journey Into Night*.

#9 Let The Music Play

Pre-show and post-show music have become standard practice in a lot of our theatre productions. In a ten-minute play festival it becomes a problem, because each director who wants music is understandably only concerned for its appropriateness to his/her play. The problem arises when the tune that's playing at the end of one play isn't appropriate to the play that follows. "Easy," you say, "just fade one song out and the other up to start the next play." True, but if you're playing music at the beginning or end of a play, you have to play enough of the music to create the effect you desire and the time between changes of plays becomes longer and longer.

My solution is real simple: no director can provide pre-show or post show music for individual plays. I use instrumental music played between each play to bridge the transitions. It's less complicated and works just as well.

#10 Do Unto Others...The Exact Same Way

Our most valuable resource in the theatre is people. We depend on the good will of those we work with to make our experiences personally satisfying and artistically rewarding. Naturally, we want everyone to feel appreciated and respected as much as we want it for ourselves. You know what your own strengths and weaknesses are as an administrator, director, producer or artistic director. What you may not be aware of is how your best intentions can create a storm of resentment and anger.

If you allow one playwright to write beyond the ten-minute mark, be prepared to do the same for all. If you turn your head the other way when one director exceeds his/her tech time by an hour, know that you'll have seven other directors who expect you to do the same for them. Look, we're human. We want to be treated fairly and equally. And when someone looks like they're getting preferential treatment, bad feelings grow like wildfire, and you can kiss the idea of "ensemble" good-bye. And that becomes just the beginning of your problems...

Ten-minute plays are a real kick in the pants when they're done well. But let's go forward with a clear head about it: shorter doesn't mean easier on any level and they're harder to produce than any of us think. When you produce them, think of a big, complicated musical – a kind of *The Color Purple* meets The Radio City Music Hall Rockettes has an affair with Edward Albee, and you'll begin to appreciate what it takes to get that goat up on its feet.

"The conflict's there – it's just hidden."

"Yes! I know, I know. It's eighteen minutes, but I took all the 'pauses' out and see, the actors don't act any faster."

"I didn't know it was supposed to be just ten pages… honest. I heard it could be, like, twenty pages if you have a really good director."

~ Three of the silliest comments I've ever heard from playwrights about their ten-minute plays.

Chapter 5

To Avoid Humiliation on Ice:

Advice From Those Who Know

Ever tried to ice skate? Remember the first time you did? I do. In two seconds this Texas boy was down for the count, my legs split in opposite directions: one leg pointing to Los Angeles and the other pointing due east, to New York. And my face had carved about a half-inch slice into the ice. My first thought was, "WOW, that hurts." My second thought was, "who saw me do that?" My third thought was, "why didn't I let her teach me a few things before I got on the ice?" My final thought was, "You're always too eager. You always jump in feet first. Could you just once wait and listen to a little simple advice?"

I think I'm a pretty smart guy. But when it comes to my writing, I always assume there are many other people so much brighter and smarter than me because they've been doing it longer, harder and with more thought. What I've learned is that if you're really smart, you figure out early on how to connect with those smarter than you and you learn from their experiences. Everybody's got a different story to tell, a different perspective, and it's all valuable to you.

I thought I'd try to save you the "ice skating" humiliation and let other people tell you what they think of the ten-minute play – what works, what doesn't and why that's important. Most things will make sense to you; maybe other things won't for now – but they will, in time, and it's all valuable.

Michael Bigelow Dixon
Former Literary Manager, Actors Theatre of Louisville

Unarguably, few theatre institutions in this country are more responsible for the development of new plays and new playwrights than Actors Theatre of Louisville. Look at a roster of their past seasons, dating back to 1976, and what you will see are the most preeminent names not only in the American theatre, but through the world. Hardly a living playwright in our day and age hasn't had at least one play developed through ATL.

Doesn't it seem almost predictable, then, that the ten-minute play would find its origins in this fertile playground for playwrights? In fact, my first memory of any notion of a "ten-minute play" for the theatre came from reading brochure copy of ATL's Humana Festival and its annual National Ten-Minute Play Contest eight years ago.

Almost synonymous with the National Ten-Minute Play Contest is the name of ATL's former Literary Manager, Michael Bigelow Dixon – a gentleman who read two-thousand-plus manuscripts a year submitted for the contest (he's since moved on to the Guthrie Theatre in Minneapolis). I had the pleasure of listening to Dixon respond to a presentation of ten-minute plays as part of the Kennedy Center's National American College Theatre Festival. What those fortunate playwrights were exposed to was a man who was not only incredibly bright, articulate and specific about what makes a successful ten-minute play, but what makes interesting, compelling theatre that engages an audience no matter the length.

GG   *Michael, why did AT institute the National 10-Minute Play Contest? Where did the idea come from?*

MBD   The National Ten-Minute Play Contest grew out of National One-Act Play Contest.

In early 1978, Jon Jory (the Producing Director of AT) through the Humana Festival was looking for a way to build relationships with prominent writers, provide opportunities for new writers with unestablished writing, find acting roles for our apprentice company and build special projects into the Humana Festival. So in 1978-79 (in the Third Annual Festival of New American Plays), we devised two projects for the Humana Festival: *Holidays* were ten ten-minute plays by American writers that were based on holidays, and featured work by playwrights such as John Glare, Marsha Norman, Israel Horovitz, Hanford Wilson, Douglas Turner Ward and Megan Terry. That (project) introduced them to ATL and the Humana Festival. What followed from there (1979-80) was *The America Project,* featuring commissioned ten-minute plays from non-USA playwrights about America, and showcased the work of Athol Fugard, Wole Solyinka, Brian Friel, Brian Clark and Carol Bolt. It was built from there and useful on four levels: it was good for the playwrights, good for the theatre, an exploration of form and it interested Jon because like the Humana Festival, it combined emerging and established writers.

GG   *Do you like them (ten-minute plays)?*

MBD   Love the ten-minute play. It's incredibly demanding and offers whatever riches you bring to it. It allows for a feeling of aesthetic eclecticism in an age where people are competing to have their voices heard. It's a real venue for multi-cultural, multi-aesthetic concerns.

GG   *Why do you think they are difficult to write?*

MBD   Because they demand complexity and success, and allow for experimentation and creative riffs. They set high standards, and since I read two thousand a year, you're very aware when the writer fulfills the potential of the story and when the writer's talent fulfills the potential of the form.

They're very fulfilling and satisfying in dimension, in form and content. Our society is experiencing a glut of stories and the ten-minute play cuts through the exposition and gets right to the conflict and change. You want to see people who are brought to the moment where they are forced to confront something that will change them or not.

GG   *I often hear the concern that focusing on such a short form will rob the writer of his/her ability to write in a longer form. Do you think that's true?*

MBD   The danger seems to be the perception that you'd be creating a David Ives instead of a Tony Kushner. They're both good writers. You could make the argument that the virtues (of writing a ten-minute play) outweigh the problems. It forces you to attend to every line, and focus on conflict and character on a moment to moment basis. I'd say its virtues are legion because if the building materials aren't compelling, it doesn't matter what length the play is.

GG   *What mistakes do you see writers make when writing the ten-minute play?*

MBD   People try to cover too much ground in the story or narrative instead of concentrating on a moment and they get to the conflict too late (longer than the first three pages). Also, they aren't ambitious enough in terms of the spiritual and metaphorical elements – that the *realistic* never transcends the mundanity of realism. The circumstance that's used is unimaginative.

GG   *A playwright friend of mine told me about your famous "point, shape and kick" prescription when writing a ten-minute play. I've never heard it, so...would you?*

MBD   "Point, shape, kick" begins with the meaning of the play – that honing and refining of what the author wants to say through the expression of the ten-minute play. What is the *point* of this and how can we maximize it in rehearsal? And because we work hands-on with our playwrights, the playwright's own thinking is part of the revision/refining process. *Shape* implies that there is some action that defines the progress of the play. It may be linear, circular, a jazz motif, anything the playwright creates. Defining the shape of the play and supporting it is a strong part of our process. And the *kick* is something that carries the play: a theatrical value, like, surprise or humor that can carry the audience's attention and evolves into satisfaction.

Russ Tutterow
Artistic Director, Chicago Dramatists

Chicago has always been a playwright's town. Visit the city on any day and you'll see a hundred different productions of original work in and around town. Many young and established writers I've known find their way to Chicago at some point or another in their careers because of the sheer volume of theatres producing new plays. It's an exciting place to be and, for playwrights, it's made easier to chase that sometime elusive dream when they're connected to an organization known as Chicago Dramatists. Formed originally in 1979 as a collective of playwrights, the group of artists eventually evolved into a theatre company that nurtures new plays and new playwrights, similar to New York City's New Dramatists. In 1986, Russ Tutterow became the artistic director of the group and has worked with hundreds of new plays and playwrights.

Chicago Dramatists has a residency program for more experienced playwrights, largely Chicago writers. The Playwrights Network – a resource for local playwrights to develop their work as playwrights – has a membership of eighty people and anyone can join it at any time. The organization offers a wide variety of playwriting classes and, four times a year, conducts a ten-minute play workshop that culminates in a staged reading for the playwright.

GG   *This is a question I'm throwing at everyone, Russ. Do you like ten-minute plays?*

RT   Love 'em.

GG   *Why?*

RT   It appeals to that area of my brain that has a short attention span. And for us (at Chicago Dramatists) it's attractive: we can work with several playwrights on one project. As a producer, to read through a whole bunch of short plays lets you get to know a lot more writers, and that's nice. Maybe even more important, though, it's getting a lot more writers on the desk of potential play buyers who are looking to keep an audience. An audience gets to see a great variety of work in a showcase, readings – whatever, and they do great by them. It's always the best audience we have. There are more people involved and they attract more people. You have, even if you do it as a rep company, each actor playing in more than one piece, so it's more fun for the actors and more fun for the audience.

GG   *Some people consider the ten-minute play a "lesser" form, an "easy workout." What do you think?*

RT   Certainly the newspaper critics that review our productions are not particularly fond of a showcase of multiple short plays. They see them as short and so look upon them as exercises, often comparing one to the other instead of looking at them for what they have to say and how each playwright says it. I don't think that's going to change as long as people consider them as minor. And critics won't ever take them seriously as long as producers don't take them seriously. Some producers will (produce ten-minute plays) to give their company a great project to work on that involves a lot of people, but they leave the people to pretty much produce them on their own, and they look slap-dash..

We discovered that – if you were going to do it right – it was very time consuming and labor intensive. Our production standards are high, even for an evening of short plays. For many years, we did a showcase of short plays as a major production, but we don't do it anymore and instead devote more time to promote more full-length play.

GG   *You're around a lot of playwrights. Does it concern you that they're spending energy and time on a short form in a way that might rob them of learning longer forms?*

RT   I don't think they take away from learning to write a longer form, no more so than a writer that works on the same play for twenty years. Television has created the short attention span and playwrights are reacting to that. Is it easier? Yes. Is it less ambitious? Yes. That doesn't necessarily make it bad.

GG   *I know you've seen your share of them, so what do you think makes for a good ten-minute play?*

RT   The most successful ten-minute play, I really believe, has all the same criteria that's in a full-length: good storytelling, character, forward motion, structure, and something wonderful. They can have big flaws, but as long as there is something wonderful about them, they'll be produced. You don't have time to develop a full story or a full character development – you don't get to develop six characters, but maybe just one. You don't have time for a main plot and two subplots – just one story that plays through.

I think a lot of people see them as "sketches." I also ask myself, is it a play or is it a review type sketch, because I've seen both. If it's a long setup and a punch line and effects a surprise at the end, that feels like a "review sketch." I guess that suggests a qualitative judgment so I guess those kinds of plays need to be in an evening of review sketches, although I've been known to mix the two in an evening.

Alexa Kelly
Artistic Director and Executive Producer,
Pulse Ensemble Theatre

Alexa Kelly has been slugging it out in New York City with her Off-Off-Broadway theatre company since 1989. Her experience with creating theatre in this city is typical to the New York scene: makes the very most of a small and somewhat inflexible performance space, operates with limited financial resources, pays for one production with another, competes with countless other theatre companies for an audience, has to nurture an acting company that also functions as stage crews and struggles to find dramatic literature that is compelling, interesting to her audience and easy to produce. But her love for the theatre, limitless energy and desire to produce thought-provoking, socially challenging theatre enables her to jump past the production obstacles and continue to produce good theatre.

Each month she produces the OPAL Series: Open Pulse Arts Lab, wherein original work, and often ten-minute plays, are produced.

GG   *What do you do think of the ten-minute play? Like them? Don't? Love them? Don't?*

AK   I like them. I think they can be a very entertaining and enlightening evening of theatre. If they're good, they can enthrall an audience by leaping about in different places and different times, taking the actors and audience on a global tour of emotional relationships. Inexperienced actors get the experience they need without torturing an audience because they can work within their scope, and whatever happens, it's only going to happen for ten minutes. And actors love them: [*Alexa groans*] they're stars for ten minutes. Young directors benefit greatly because they (the plays) have to be about something dramatically, and be quick about it. The director has to learn to build an emotional life into the play – almost lightning-fast – then add more life to it as it goes.

The audience is always surprised by how much fun the evening can be because I don't think they come with the idea that they are going to be emotionally engaged, and they're surprised when they discover they are. And if they're not, nothing goes on too long for them. If they find they don't like a play, it's only a matter of a few minutes before it's over.

GG   *Any advice you'd give writers?*

AK   I don't always care for one-acts or short plays because they rarely, if ever, feel complete.

But if you write a good ten-minute play, it has a point to make and it makes it in a way that feels full. The story may be small, or normal, but the issue is huge – so big that it surprises everyone. It doesn't wander around (there's no time), trying to find its story or conflict.

And I think the plays that work best in this kind of theatre don't have a beginning – just a middle and end. They (the playwrights) should plunge into the very middle of a dramatic situation because the beginning can be implicit in the story if it's written well. Let the beginning happen offstage and drop us into a world that is conflicted already. We don't have time to draw the audience in slowly; they have to comprehend what's at stake immediately and care about it from the moment the lights come up.

For my tastes, they should have a little emotional surprise to them. You shouldn't know what they're about – not really, not completely. There should be something very normal about the story, immediately, and then it works well if it has a surprise emotional twist that slowly reveals itself. And that takes you aback when you realize there's a huge scope to what seemed to be a very simple story. And the audience loves – *they love it* – when they think something is about one thing and it turns out it's about something else.

GG *I think they're hard to produce. I think, whatta headache. You?*

AK (*she laughs*) I think they're much easier to produce than full length plays. Yes, there's double of everything to do. And it takes more organizational ability on the whole structure of the evening to make it work. But we have more playwrights, directors and actors – more people – to make it work and who bring more people into the theatre because they're involved. You're not playing on any famous name playwright or director, usually, and the actors are the actors you always work with, so that means you can keep everything simple – it has to be about the actors and the story. And if that's the case, you can use six black chairs, two black tables, and two black cubes and create the world of the play with good writing and acting. That's what we do in the Opal Series.

GG *Just six black chairs, huh? Hmmmm.*

AK Yes, believe it or not, you can create a world (*she laughs*) despite the lack of furniture.

Laura Margolis
Producing Manager, StageWorks

If Alexa Kelly and Pulse Ensemble Theatre is typical of the perennially struggling Off-Off-Broadway theatre company, Laura Margolis and StageWorks is typical of the perennially struggling small professional theatre company outside of a larger metropolitan city. Situated in the city of Hudson just outside of Albany in upstate New York, StageWorks cultivates an audience from a hundred mile radius of their performance facility. Laura spends eight months of the year preparing for her four-month season, spanning May to August. For the last four years, StageWorks has produced an annual festival of ten-minute plays, "Ten by Ten," thematically centered on one primary color: purple, blue, red, etc.

GG: *How did that color thing get started?*

LM   Honestly? We thought it was great way to meet a lot of new writers and to offer something different than just your typical festival of plays. We put together a *Ten by Ten* committee of theatre and literary professionals, so that they could be charged with reading all the plays and selecting them. When the committee got together, I suggested as the producer that it would more interesting – to my mind – if there was something that tied them together thematically, yet left the writer a lot of room for creativity. We talked about a lot of different things, but the [thematic] use of color seemed to be the most freeing. It was general and yet specific enough to ignite the imagination of the playwright. So far we've done red, green, purple and black/white.

The first year we presented them as readings in a rough, rough workshop style as a supplement to our mainstage season. They were directed and up on their feet, book in hand. They were overwhelmingly (and almost immediately) popular because it seems that the audience – aside from the writing – enjoyed the search for the color in the course of the play. I know that sounds crazy, but it's true. There's this weird element of, where is the color? So in some subliminal or even obvious way, the color ties the evening together and the audience is sort of tricked into taking the ride.

I love the ten-minute play. I feel as a theater artist, that we often trap ourselves by what we perceive as limitations. But with any limitation in the theatre, there is immense creative freedom.

A whole explosion of creativity is going to open to you when you limit the world you're writing about to an elevator. But if you put your world in the middle of Grand Central Station, it's less interesting. You've got rules and regulations everywhere in your life, and we all understand that. So in this, you've got ten minutes to explode creatively, and that's just what you should do.

GG   *Writing this book, I'm in that search, that, looking-for-an-answer kind of place where I'm trying to figure out what makes an interesting ten-minute play. I'm shy to say a "good" ten-minute play because that's so subjective. But I bet you're not shy about it. So what makes a good ten-minute play?*

LM   That's easy. We're looking for what I think everyone else is looking for: a great, compelling story with compelling characters that in ten minutes creates a wonderful theatre experience – it takes us on a journey that deals with circumstances that are identifiable to us emotionally. It's the same stuff of a longer play, only shorter and they jump from the beginning. There's a green light from the moment the play starts that nudges the story to dash out of the starting gate, like, go, go, go. Yeah, I'd say that's one of the key features of a good ten minute: the green light.

    That's for the writer. As producers, we need to put together an evening that is diverse, has a variety of writing styles and approaches to the idea of theatre that stimulates everyone's imagination. Then we get very, uhm, *dry* – for lack of a better word – about our practicalities of production. For example, we limit the cast size to four because we pull the whole evening off with only six actors – partly for us, because it works with the practical realities we face of producing theatre with limited resources, and partly for the audience because it's clear they have fun watching six actors play twenty-five roles. The audience gets to see actors play a huge span of different characters. It's like the old repertory theatre audience; an actor plays a variety of roles throughout the season, but here they see it in one evening.

    Producing it requires a whole different head, another way of thinking about your production. You need to have some thought about the transitions and transformation from one play to another, and at the same time, keep the arc of the entire evening in mind. An audience – just like in a full-length play – needs a through line that pulls them through a dramatically compelling evening.

This inevitably leads to a discussion of what play to start with, what play to end with, what play(s) should be in the middle. Do you begin and end with the comedies or the dramas? How do we arrange the evening so that the small group of actors we're using aren't working in plays back to back, exhausting them?

GG   *A lot of work, huh?*

LM   Yeah, but fun work. It's like a jig-saw puzzle. But every year after the production comes down, we've figured out a way to do it more simply for the next year. Each year we're so excited, frankly, that we've figured out how to produce it. It's an achievement. Each year it's all different: the set, the concept, the writers. We create an environment for it all to happen...and it happens, with a lot of work...and I guess, a little bit of...I don't know, can I say, magic?

B. J. Scott
Artistic Director, Camino Real Playhouse

Like any snotty east coast theatre person, I sometimes indulge in those little jabs we all take at the west coast for their supposed lack of good theatre. The truth of the matter is that extraordinarily vital, important theatre is being done up and down the west coast. B. J. Scott's small theatre in San Juan Capistrano, California, works hard to engage its local audience with theatre that is both meaningful and entertaining. Camino Real Playhouse has been around for twelve years and has produced eight seasons of theatre. Situated in a Catholic neighborhood, the theatre has to – by necessity – be family-oriented and conscious about being politically correct – no small task as each year they produce the *Show Off Playwriting Festival,* which solicits submissions for ten-minute plays. This year they received four hundred and fifty submissions.

GG   *So out of that four hundred and fifty submissions, how do you decide which to produce?*

BJS   Our main focus is that we find something that will make for an entertaining evening. So we look for something unusual, something different. What we *don't* spend a lot of time reading are the boy meets girl, loses girl, gets girl back kind of play. Or the blind date play – you know, where two people meet in a restaurant. They're so predictable, and I guess we're more drawn to anything that's not (predictable). Oh, and the sit-com scenario doesn't get very far with us – that one-joke plot thing. Unfortunately, about ninety percent of what we read are those kinds of plays.

GG *So I take it you've read a few bad ten-minute plays?*

BJS Yeah, but it's not that the writing is so bad, story to story, it's the lack of an interesting idea in these plays that's so frustrating. When the idea isn't there, quite often there's no character either, or no real story. I guess what I'm really saying is that there has to be a good idea behind the play with characters and a story that supports it. And you have to get to it really quickly – kinda like, you know, haiku for the theatre. It has to happen on the first page, not the last.

And writers get in their own way, sometimes. They, like, *require* that their plays have a cast of ten. No. I can't do it. There's a comfort level to consider when you have thirty people back stage and your theatre's designed to only have ten. Or a writer will create a character that has to be extremely obese. Well, I don't know that many extremely obese actors, so right away I'm limited. Which doesn't mean you shouldn't write the play you want to write, but you do have to remember that I have to produce it. And yes, we've got plenty of actors around, but I don't always know if I can find three black actors and two Asian actresses in order to produce your play. I'll always try, but I also have to remember who I have to play with. Sometimes it all comes down to just that: who do I know that can play these characters? I'm one to keep it as simple as possible.

GG *Actors really seem to like to work on ten-minute plays. Is that your experience?*

BJS Absolutely, it's attractive to a lot of professional actors because it's not a huge commitment. I know actors who won't audition for a regular play, but will audition for the ten-minute play festival because you rehearse it eight times and you're up. You can bank on a short time period and you don't have to learn a jillion lines. Actually, it's very time-efficient for each of the creative components

because there's not all of the stuff that goes into a full production
– the long technical rehearsals, changing costumes three or four
times because you're changing seasons three or four times. With a
ten-minute play, it's more immediate – it's more of the moment.

GG *And your audiences like them?*

BJS The audiences love them. Don't get me wrong, they don't appeal
to everyone, but most people who see them, like them. And the
press eats it up. It's giving new writers a forum because these
are playwrights that might not be heard otherwise. And it's all so
varied. You can watch one that you really hate and know you're
not trapped in the theatre because in ten minutes it'll all be over.
That's not so bad.

Gregg Henry
Artistic Director, The John F. Kennedy Center's
American College Theatre Festival

Gregg came into his position of Artistic Director for the Kennedy
Center's American College Theatre Festival (KC/ACTF), having served
in his own region of the country (the Midwest) for several years as its
regional chair for KC/ACTF. In his region, Gregg was responsible for
programming at the regional festival wherein hundreds of student actors,
directors, playwrights and designers gathered to celebrate the college
theatre of that region. Now, in his new position, not only does he do the
same for the national festival held each year in Washington, D.C., but he's
responsible for the almost bursting-at-the-seams opportunities afforded
student playwrights as part of the Kennedy Center's educational mission.
One such opportunity was the inauguration and development of a student
National Ten-Minute Play Festival that's heading into its third year.

GG *The Kennedy Center's American College Theatre Festival took a
big step several years ago by instituting a National Ten-Minute
Play Festival. Why do you think they got behind it?*

GH   I can't speculate why it moved (from the regions) to Washington (and the National Festival) so fast. I think it would be safe to say that what we saw happening at the regional level was an incredible opportunity for playwrights to write in a difficult but manageable form and – long story short – see their work performed at a festival of new works. The other benefit, of course, was the collaborative opportunities. I think what we came to understand was we had a project where strangers (actors, playwrights and directors) would be thrown together and by the end of x period, they would bond and make something happen. That's the ACTF phenomena when we're doing it right: building and sharing things together. So for us, it really serves two functions: it furthers the unspoken mission in that it introduces young artists to one another and it provides young artists with some pretty essential theatre tools.

GG   *I know you have some...difficulties...with the whole notion of a ten-minute play. Want to share?*

GH   Reservations...hhhmmmm. What are they? Well, first is form: I think when they're done well, and right, they're a terrific tool or exercise in having the playwright understand (dramatic) structure. Bang, lay out the facts, crash, get the complications in there and resolve what's done. The whole thing should be this complete, tight theatre experience. But that's not what happens a lot of the time. What I see are *not* ten-minute plays; they're scenes. Last year, I was a respondent to a bill of ten-minute plays, and I heard myself keep saying, "this is not a ten-minute play, because I want to know more about this person and more about what it's about," because what *was there* felt so incomplete. Like, I kept seeing character studies that were charming, but I didn't think the characters were a complete entity.

Another worry is that it's too easy to fall into a 'this is quick and easy" kind of mentality, and then what you get are a lot of reviews or Saturday Night Live sketches. The ten-minute restriction plucks at the attention span – which we know is about a steady seven minutes in the entertainment field. That's what television commercials have done for us. And I also worry that some think "I can do this," but they don't take the next step of learning a fuller form.

I think ten-minute plays teach structure, and that's a good thing, but they come with their share of bad writer-things. I'm not saying let's adhere to the (Aristotle's) *Poetics*, but longer forms give the playwright time to lay out the givens; a little more leisure time to lay out the exposition and that crack of inciting incident. Too often (with a ten-minute play), somebody is getting rewarded for writing a sketch, which might be the right length, but is not a play.

GG   *You've long been an actor, theatre director, administrator and acting teacher. Are there problems that you see with ten-minute plays that tend to trip up the actor? Or better yet, what actor problems inevitably reveal themselves when an actor is working on a ten-minute play?*

GH   Just as I think it is great tool for a writer, particularly when it comes to establishing character quickly and getting the necessary emotional information across to the audience efficiently, I think it's a great tool for the actor because they have to do the exact same thing. I have always been a cheerleader for big, strong, bold choices, and a ten-minute play allows the actors just that. They don't have the luxury of time. You walk on stage and something has to be emanating out of every pore of your person. (Jon) Jory (Actors Theatre of Louisville) says the play starts with a lightning bolt; both actors and directors need to learn that. How do you grab, and how do you hold?

I always get a case of blue balls when I work on a scene with student actors because I always find myself saying, "Oh, do you know what comes next," or "Do you know what came before it," because there's always something before or after a scene in a longer play. But I found myself assigning and recommending ten minute plays in directing class because if it's a good ten minute play, there's a sense of satisfaction because we have seen it all – you can find the mechanism of the whole thing.

GG   *Think they'll be around for a while? Or is it all just a passing fancy?*

GH   I think they'll be around for a long while. I do. I think, too, the more I read the collections, the more I see people understand now what they can do, what they can be and what they can accomplish. More and more playwrights seem to have a Jory lightning bolt after lightning bolt and produce these beautiful poetic jewels. And if the writer does his job, it's whole and satisfying. But I still need my *Arcadia*s that take their time, make me laugh and cry in a full evening. I still like myself to be engaged over a longer period of time.

Judith Royer
Playwrights Program,
Association for Theatre in Higher Education

Interviewing Judith, I have a quadruple resource: not only is she a free-lance director who's worked with countless playwrights developing their plays through production, but she's also a professor of acting and directing at Loyola Marymount University in Los Angeles, as well as serving for years in a leadership position in the Playwrights Program of the Association for Theatre in Higher Education (a service organization that brings academics/artists together by discipline). And as if that didn't provide her enough new plays to work on, she has been the west coast's regional chair for the National Playwriting Program of the Kennedy Center's American College Theatre Program (which brings together student playwrights). Here is a woman with extraordinary experience with new plays written by playwrights that span all ages, cultural backgrounds, varieties of education and professional affiliations. And lucky for all of us, Judith has fostered the development of the ten-minute play not only in her region of the country, but throughout the United States through her affiliation with the Kennedy Center.

GG   *You've worked with so many different kinds of playwrights, from so many different backgrounds and abilities. And I know I've been witness to your witnessing of hundreds of ten- minute plays. Is there any one universal truth that resonates in you about the whole of it?*

JR   We all seem to underestimate what a difficult form it is and forget that we can't treat it like a sketch. It's a much more difficult form because it has to have everything a long play has with the same clarity of action. I see a lot of character studies that try to be ten-minute plays, and they're interesting, but they're little more than character sketches for a longer play.

The trick is to find an action line that pays off in some meaningful way. And I know how hard that is – for young writers and old. But I also know that we foster a lot of ten-minute plays that haven't hit the mark yet because we often want to foster the playwright (just not necessarily the play). The ten-minute play seems to be an ideal form to encourage and support the less experienced writer because it's challenging, but manageable.

GG   *So they're a good thing for writers?*

JR   For the experience of learning their craft, yes. But they need to be kicked beyond that. I see a lot of MFA writing programs using the form to teach, and that's great. But in the professional theatre, we're ending up with submissions that are just collections of ten-minute plays. I see plenty of writers who can handle the ten-minute form but can't write a longer play; they can't sustain a multi-faceted story and instead just write a lot of ambiance and dialogue.

As an acting teacher, they're wonderful for young actors because they're not taking cuttings from longer plays that you're not sure they fully understand anyway. Student actors can handle the form if it's well written and brings together all the good elements of drama. And for young directing students, it's a perfect teaching tool because, again, it's manageable. As a director myself, it's more of an exercise than anything else. You're literally hitting that action line and going with it, and that's it. You just clarify that action line. There's never much rehearsal time, so you let your actors take their own leads and let them go.

GG   *Okay, so I'm gonna skip over the "do you like them" kind of questions, because frankly it seems that everybody likes them. Here's my question to you: what don't you like about them?*

JR   (laughing) The fact that you don't see many good ones.

GG   *Why do you think?*

JR   Some writers are literally only interested in how clever they can turn the ending or the initial assumption: God and the Devil caught in an elevator, going up and down between Heaven and Hell. That's the device. Somehow there has to be something that will grab you on a level that isn't just clever, and that can still go somewhere in ten minutes.

For the writer, there is no time to develop much character; subtlety and complexity is hard to pull off in ten-minutes but is so needed. And when it is written with subtlety and complexity, I don't know that directors and actors can pull it off because there's usually never much time to rehearse them. Everyone underestimates the process, and it becomes all about getting it up. And the really good ten-minute plays need time. I've spent more time on a four-minute piece than a twenty-minute piece because with less material, there's more to bring to life. And because it's really, really short, you either you hit the first beat, or you never get there. Either you jump on the roller coaster or not.

GG *What's your biggest headache when you go about producing a bill of ten-minute plays, even if it's just for a sit-down reading?*

JR Personnel. Specifically directors. No matter how well you think you've selected, how many resumes you've looked at, how many people you've talked to, I've found if there's a consistent problem in production, it's usually with a director, or more specifically, a director's ego. Let's face it: a lot of people don't know how to work with this format, or with new, original work and playwrights. There's so little time – literally – in both the production and the play, and I see a lot of directors that don't know how to get out of the way of the material because their own egos are involved. They burden the plays with too much attention. They see it as, they've only got ten minutes to make their mark, and they're so afraid that if they haven't staged it brilliantly, it reflects on them.

They should clarify the story with the writer and actors and just make sure the story's being told. And that's a very special skill. A full-length play doesn't afford them the time to focus so intensely and almost unrelentingly on its presentation. And when they do that with a ten-minute play, you hear about hours and hours of rehearsal scheduled because they (the director) are looking a this little moment and that little moment, and the plays suddenly become double their actual length.

GG *Any last thoughts?*

JR It's a consummate art, when you think about it.

...now what?

~ Michel Wallerstein, playwright,
on finishing a ten-minute play

CHAPTER 6

Drying Out Your Mouth

You're finished. Done. You've read it ten times since writing "lights fade," re-read it again with emotions, without emotions, with accents, without the accents, laughed at your own jokes and assured yourself that Uncle Donnie *could not, would not*, without a shadow of a doubt, fall asleep during this play. You've saved the computer file on eight different disks and made five paper copies: one you put in the freezer in case the apartment catches fire, one you mailed to yourself for copyright purposes, one you gave to your best friend to read cause she'll love it, one you gave to your teacher cause he'll hate it and you need that punishment to keep you writing well and one you've kept on your desk as a symbol of "see, I can finish something."

Now what?

Big question. Big ol' empty, frustrating, confounding question – *because who's really going to produce a ten-minute play anyway*, you think? Your mouth instantly dries out: is it anxiety because you don't know what to do, where to send your play, or is it the anticipation of licking stamps for the Self-Addressed-Stamped-Envelope? Here's the good news: that dry mouth syndrome is now easily remedied.

First, most theatres don't want you to send a SASE because they won't/ can't/don't want to return your play – it's too much of an administrative headache for the volume of work they receive. Second: there are scores of places that are looking for short plays, monologue plays and ten-minute plays. Every day a new theatre discovers the benefits of producing an evening of ten-minute plays. Every day colleges and universities, drama clubs and small groups of actors all stumble on the joy of creating a night of different voices with intriguing view points on issues that concern their audience. You shouldn't have trouble finding a place to send your ten-minute play, but you might have trouble getting them to read it if you don't follow a few simple suggestions and acknowledge a few realities:

1. There are too many of us (playwrights) and too few of them (theatres who routinely produce new original work). Your first job, then, is to make your work known in such a way as to invite not only the submission of your current play, but any other work you might

have. This starts with taking the time to *research* where and how to submit your play and then *believing* and honoring your research.

If you read the *Dramatists Guild Resource Guide* or the TCG *Dramatists Sourcebook,* and the description in a submission process notes that the theatre is not looking for kitchen realism, *believe it.* If the description says that you should submit from January to May, *believe it.* If the description says that it'll take six months for a response, *believe it* (then add two additional months). If the description says, "plays for women by women," *believe it.* If the description requests a synopsis, don't try to forget that you read that and hope they won't notice it's missing from your package. If the solicitation description says that the company is looking for plays with six characters or under, why would you send a play with nine? Do you think they won't see the other three? Or do you think that they'll be so taken with your play that the three additional characters won't matter? *BELIEVE IT – they want six or under!* Every artistic director and literary manager that I've had the pleasure of doing business with remarks consistently that writers either don't read, believe or honor their submission descriptions.

2. Submit what the theatre asks for, nothing more, nothing less, *and make it easy for them.* This is particularly true when there's a page number limit or a character limit. Remember, you're trying to sell them something on their time. So if a theater is asking for play that's no more than ten pages and has four characters or fewer, don't waste your time or theirs if your play doesn't match that description.

    What's included in a submission package is a letter of introduction followed by either a resume, a synopsis, and/or the full text. This means you have to learn to write a business letter of introduction that (a) isn't cute, (b) isn't rambling, (c) isn't bitter, and (d) isn't so long that they might as well have read the play, but is (e) short, direct, acknowledges their particular interests and why your play is suitable for their consideration.

    This introductory letter is their first exposure to your writing. Don't blow it off because it's only a letter. It should simply state that you're responding to their solicitation for ten-minute plays in blah-blah-blah magazine or journal, that you're enclosing a copy of your play (share the title), and then briefly describe the story of the play using every creative writing skill you've ever been taught. Seduce the reader into wanting to want to read the play, but keep it short.

Something to avoid in your letter: *"This is an uproarious comedy... this is a heart-breaking account of..."* Let someone else be the judge. If you have any questions about your description, give it to somebody who knows your play and ask for a fair assessment. You didn't write your play without feedback, why chance the description?

3. A full-text submission should be either stapled or hole-punched and braded or secured in a thin folder. Never use paper clips: they fall off. And don't waste your money on a sturdy binder. They take up too much room. Above all else, make sure your page numbers are visibly printed.

   The first page of your manuscript is a cover page with your name, address, phone number and e-mail address, followed by a character breakdown on a separate page that specifies the character names, age, sex and a brief description of who they are. The text follows after that. And just so we're all clear about this: the first page of your play with action and dialogue is Page 1 – not the cover page or character breakdown.

   I've seen so many plays ignored, dismissed and refused to be read because the playwright didn't follow the simple rule of submission. Don't do that to yourself. Celebrate what you've written and try to share it with the rest of the world.

On the following pages are sixty-four theatres and producing organizations that are looking specifically for ten-minute plays. I've left some of the submission dates off some of the entries because these dates often change (if it's not an established festival or theatre). These are at the end of the section, as the list is in order by deadline date. Go to the website listed, or Google the theatre or production company to get the most recent deadline listing. Finally, pay particular attention to what these potential opportunities ask for with specifics to style and genre.

Inspirato Festival, Toronto Ten Minute Play Festival
Inspirato Festival
www.inspiratofestival.ca
http://www.inspiratofestival.ca/write-a-play.php

> **Consideration.** Remuneration: $100, production.
>
> **Preference.** Length: 8-12 minutes. Content/Subject Matter: sense of smell must be an important element of your play.
>
> **Application.** See website for online submission (www.inspiratofestival.ca/write-a-play2.php). Attach script in a WORD Document. The cover page should only have the title of the play, the playwright's name and the list of characters. The pages should be numbered. Deadline: January 4.

Kingwood College Theatre's Annual Evening Of One-Act Plays
Eric C. Skiles, Artistic Director of Theatre
Kingwood College
20000 Kingwood Dr., Office 104C, Kingwood, TX 77339
281-312-1672
eric.c.skiles@nhmccd.edu

> **Consideration.** Production
>
> **Application.** Submit one copy of your play and contact information. The selected plays will be produced by Kingwood College. Plays will be selected anonymously by committee – ALL playwrights will be notified by February. Plays will be directed, designed, and acted by Students/Community Members. Playwrights will receive programs, production photos, and feedback from directors, designers, and actors. Deadline: January 15.

EstroGenius
Estrogenius Short Play Showcase
manhattantheatresource
177 MacDougal St., New York, NY 10011
estrogenius.festival@gmail.com
www.estrogenius.org

> **Preferences**. New short plays by female writers, no monologues. Length: 10-15 minutes. Simple production values.
>
> **Application**: see website for "cover sheet." Submit play, completed cover sheet, and character breakdown to manhattantheatresource, Attn: Estrogenius Short Play Showcase - play selection, 177 MacDougal St., New York, NY 10011. Deadline: January 15 - March 15, 2009.

The Arts Center
10 by 10 in the Triangle
300-G East Main St., Carrboro, NC 27510
919-929-2787
infor@artscenterlive.org
www.artscenterlive.org

> **Remuneration:** $100 plus travel stipend.
>
> **Preference.** 10 minute plays.
>
> **Application.** For each play, send two separate emails to theatre@ artscenterlive.org. The first e-mail regards playwright contact information and the second regards contents of the play. **E-mail 1** – the subject line and the attached file retain the same name, which is the title of the play followed by the phrase "contact info." For example, if the name of the play is *Poker Face*, the subject line and attached file would read "Poker Face contact info". The attached file only contains the title page with contact information. Please use the full title of the play as numerous plays with similar titles are often received. **Email 2** – the subject line and the attached file retain the same name, which is the title of the play. For example, the subject line of this email is Poker Face and the attached file is Poker Face. This file contains cast, set requirements, and script. No contact information, please. If you are submitting two scripts, please send four separate emails. Please do not zip the files. Submission period: January-February 15, 2009.

Little Fish Theatre
Pick of the Vine
www.littlefishtheatre.org

> **Preference.** Minimal set requirements, 6 or fewer characters.
>
> **Application.** Email script with contact info to melanie@littlefishtheatre. org or mail hard copy to: Melanie Jones , Little Fish Theatre, 619 West 38th St, San Pedro CA 90731. http://www.littlefishtheatre.org/scripts. html. Deadline: January/February.

Heartland Theatre Company
P. O. Box 1833, Bloomington, IL 61702
(Attention: Play Fest)
playfest@heartlandtheatre.org
www.heartlandtheatre.org
www.heartlandtheatre.org/tenminute_rules.html

> **Consideration.** Eight short original plays to be considered for production.

Preference. Length: Keep it TEN MINUTES long (approx. ten pages) and in English. Keep in mind the physical space at Heartland. Remember something has to happen in those ten minutes. Content/ Subject Matter: Stick with the theme of given year (check website). Please use no more than four characters, and no fewer than 2. Characters should stay within the 18-70 age range. No ten-minute monologues, please. One submission per author.

Application. All applicants must send a signed copy of the Entry Form to Heartland Theatre Company, available in PDF (online fill-in) or MSWord format. No scripts will be returned. Title page must include name, address, phone number and e-mail of author. No plays previously submitted to Heartland Theatre Company, no children's plays, no musicals, no previous staged productions. We'll also need a brief summary or "blurb" of your play to help our readers as well as smooth the way for auditions and advertising if your play is produced. Please include this summary – one paragraph, no more than 50 words – after your cover page but before your script. Winners will be posted on the Heartland website. Deadline: February 1.

Art Work Enterprises
Rogue Valley 10-Minute Plays Festival
www.ashlandnewplays.org
www.ashlandnewplays.org/participate-tmpf-playwrights.html

Consideration. Production and development.

Preference. Length: 12 pages or less

Application. E-mail script as pdf or word file with a subject line of "TMPF Submission" to info@AshlandNewPlays.org. Deadline: February 1- May 1

Rochester Repertory Theatre
Rochester Repertory Ten Minute Play Competition
Ten Minute Play Competition
Rochester Repertory Theatre
103 7th St. N.E., Rochester, MN 55906
boxoffice@rochesterrep.org
www.rochesterrep.org

Preference. Length: at least 10 minutes. Production: minimal production requirements. Content/Subject Matter: "Glass Half Full." Material Must Be: unproduced, not a translation or adaptation.

Application. Submit play to Ten Minute Play Competition, Rochester Repertory Theatre, 103 7th St. N.E., Rochester, MN 55906.

Title page should include the play's title, playwright's name, e-mail, address and telephone number. No name on manuscript. Title page should not be attached to the rest of the script. The title of the script should appear on each page of the script along with page numbering. Deadline: February 5th.

Theatre Oxford
10 Minute Play Contest
P. O. Box 1321, Oxford, MS 38655
Contact: Dinah Swan, Contest Director, 662-236-5052
http://www.10minuteplays.com/

Consideration. Five winners will be chosen. The Grand Prize Winner will receive the L. W. Thomas Award and $1,000, a later production of the winning entry by Theatre Oxford, opening night's lodging, and lunch for two.

Preference. Each playwright may submit only ONE play (typed, no emails or disks) Length: Maybe no more than ten pages. Only original plays, never before produced, are eligible.

Application. Assemble script as follows: Optional cover letter; a title page with the play's title, author's name, address, phone number, and email address. (This is the only place the author's name should appear.) The second page should contain a cast of characters list and time and place information. Do not include a synopsis or any directorial information. The third page will be the first page of the script. Write the play's title at the top of this page. The other pages of the play follow. Staple or paper clip the play. Do NOT use binders or folders of any kind. Plays cannot be returned. Enclose a SASP if you want assurance that your play was received. Deadline: February 15. Submissions must be postmarked on or before deadline. No exceptions. This contest requires a submission fee. Check the website for details.

Princeton University Ten-Minute Play Contest
Theater and Dance Program
185 Nassau St., Princeton University, Princeton NJ 08544
609-258-8562
http://www.princeton.edu/~visarts/tenminply.htm

Consideration: Youth award. Remuneration: First Prize: $500; Second Prize: $250; Third Prize: $100.

Preference. Length: 10-Minute. Author Must Be: Any student who is in the eleventh grade.

Application. Submit one copy of play, include name, address, and phone number on submission and online form, www.princeton. edu/~visarts/tenminply.htm. Submit to: Princeton Ten-Minute Play Contest, Theater and Dance Program, 185 Nassau Street, Princeton University, Princeton NJ 08544. Deadline: March 1, postmarked.

Fire Rose Productions
10-Minute International Play Competition
11246 Magnolia Blvd., NoHo Theatre & Arts District, CA 91601
818-766-3691
info@fir500roseproductions.com

info@fireroseproductions.com
www.fireroseproductions.com

> **Consideration.** Fees: $5 each play. Remuneration: production, cash prize.
>
> **Preference.** Length: 10 minutes.
>
> **Application.** Submit unbound play, fee, and application (see website) to 10-Minute Play Competition, Fire Rose Productions, 11246 Magnolia Blvd., NoHo Theatre & Arts District, CA 91601. Deadline: March 2009, postmarked.

Arena Stage
The Student Playwrights Project
Arena Stage – Community Engagement Division
1101 Sixth Street, SW, Washington, DC 20024
202-234-5782
education@arenastage.org
www.arenastage.org

> **Consideration**: youth competition.
>
> **Preference.** Length: 6-12 pages. Author Must Be: students between 5th and 12th grades and attend school in the District of Columbia, the City of Alexandria, or one of the following counties: Loudoun, Prince Georges, Prince William, Montgomery, Fairfax or Arlington. Home school students must be a resident of D.C., Alexandria or one of the listed counties. Material Must Be: original, unpublished work of one playwright.
>
> **Application.** Submit three copies of the entered play. List on entry: full name, date of birth, grade, school, home address, home phone, school address, school phone, teacher's name and principal's name. Submit to: Student Playwrights Project, Arena Stage – Community Engagement Division, 1101 Sixth Street, SW, Washington, DC 20024. Deadline: postmarked or received by March 12

The Eclectic Theatre Company
Hurricane Season Playwriting Competition
5312 Laurel Canyon Blvd., Valley Village, CA 91607
818-508-3003
www.hurricaneseasontheatre.com

Consideration. Fees: $10 before Feb 15, $15 before March 15 (processing fee). Remuneration: (6) $75 prizes will be awarded to semi-finalists restaged in the 5th or 6th weekend, (3) $125 prizes (in addition to other winnings) will be awarded to finalists restaged in the 7th weekend, (1) $500 prize (in addition to other winnings) will be awarded as determined by audience voting of the 7th weekend.

Preference. Length: 15-35 minutes. Minimal set. No one-person plays. Material Must Be: unpublished, unproduced in California.

Application. Submit two (2) paper copies of your script (no personal info on the script), accompanied by a cover letter that includes name, address, phone number, e-mail, and source along with a check payable to The Eclectic Company Theatre. Submit to: Hurricane Season 2008, c/o The Eclectic Company Theatre, 5312 Laurel Canyon Blvd., Valley Village, CA 91607 Deadline: March 15, 2008.

Theatre Limina
"Summer Shorts" Festival
www.theatrelimina.org

Consideration. Production.

Preference. Length: 20 minutes. Production: 4 actors or fewer. Content/Subject Matter: theme for 2008 is "Summer Shorts: Bermuda Shorts."

Application. Include two electronic copies of each script in Microsoft Word format (.doc) as e-mail attachments, one bearing your name and contact information, the other completely devoid of any identifying information. In the text of the e-mail message, include performance history for each script. If desired, include a brief statement about yourself as a playwright and what you hope to extract from this experience.

Application. Eric Nelson at SummerShorts08@gmail.com. Deadline: March 30th.

Hunger Artists Theatre Company
Beyond Convention
699-A S. State College Blvd., Fullerton, California 92831
714-680-6803
beyondconvention@gmail.com
www.hungerartists.com

> **Consideration.** Remuneration: production.
>
> **Preference.** Length: approximately ten minutes. Content/Subject Matter: challenge normal theatre conventions
>
> **Application.** Submit script (a doc or pdf), a cast list, title page including your contact information, and bio to beyondconvention@gmail.com. Deadline: March 31.

Theatre Southwest
Festival of Originals
944 Clarkcrest, Houston, Texas 77063
www.theatresouthwest.org
http://www.theatresouthwest.org/pages/submissions.htm

> **Consideration**. Remuneration: production, $100.
>
> **Preference**. No Monologues. Length: 20 minutes. Material Must Be: unproduced.
>
> **Application**. Submit script, fee, plot summary to Theatre Southwest, 944 Clarkcrest, Houston, Texas 77063, Attention: Festival Submissions; or email mimi@theatresouthwest.org. Deadline: April 1.

Playwrights Foundation
BASH! (Bay Area Shorts)
131 10th St., San Francisco, CA 94103
Beth Given, Literary Intern
Beth@laywrightsfoundation.org
www.playwrightsfoundation.org

> **Consideration.** mentorship, reading.
>
> **Preference.** Length: 20-minute plays/excerpts only. Author Must Be: residing in the Bay Area.
>
> **Application.** Submit play to BASH! 2008, Playwrights Foundation, 131 10th St., San Francisco, CA 94103. Deadline: April 1st

EATheatre, Emerging Artists Theatre
EATfest
464 W. 25th St. #4, New York, NY 10001-6501
212-247-2429
www.eatheatre.org
http://www.EATheatre.org/submissions.php

> **Consideration.** Remuneration: production.
>
> **Preferences.** No monologues. Length: 10 to 20 minutes. Material Must Be: unproduced in NYC , unpublished.
>
> **Application.** Submit online via website (preferred), or send play to Emerging Artists Theatre, Attention: Playwrights Manager, 464 W. 25th St. #4, New York, NY 10001-6501. Include play and a letter including your name, telephone number, address and e-mail address. Deadline: April 1.

Salem Theatre Company
Moments of Play: A Festival of One-Acts
Catherine Bertrand
978-790-8546
info@salemtheatre.com
www.salemtheatre.com

> **Consideration.** Remuneration: production only.
>
> **Preference.** Length: not be longer than 10 minutes. Minimal scene set up.
>
> **Application.** Submit the play, brief synopsis not exceeding one page, and character breakdown to: info@salemtheatre.com; or mail to P.O. Box 306, Salem, MA 01970. Deadline: April 2.

Rapscallion Theatre Collective
Salute UR Shorts New Play Festival
1111 Putnam Ave #2, Brooklyn, NY 11221
rapscalliontheatre@gmail.com
www.rapscalliontheatrecollective.com

> **Consideration:** production.
>
> **Preference.** Length: 10-15 minutes
>
> **Application.** Submit play to rapscalliontheatre@gmail.com (preferred method), or mail to 1111 Putnam Ave #2, attn: Rey Hewitt, Brooklyn, NY 11221. Deadline: April 15th

The Department of Theatre, SUNY College at Brockport
Biennial Festival of Ten-Minute Plays
gmusante@brockport.edu
http://www.brockport.edu/theatre

> **Consideration.** Fees: An entry fee of $3.00 for each submitted script must be included; $1 per play for full-time students. Make checks out to: SUNY Brockport, Department of Theatre. Remuneration: production and cash prizes for top three plays ($300, $200, $100).

> **Preference.** Length: 7-12 minutes.

> **Application.** See website. Submit two copies of unbound script, fastened in upper left-hand corner only. The play title must appear on each page, the playwright's name must not appear anywhere on the script. A "blind" title page, containing title only, must be attached to the script. An additional, removable cover page must contain: title, name of playwright, mailing address, telephone number, email address. Submit to: New Plays VI, Department of Theatre, SUNY College at Brockport, 350 New Campus Drive, Brockport, NY 14420. Deadline: April 26.

Augustana College and The Great Plains Dramatist Exchange
'8 in 48:' Claire Donaldson Short Play Festival
haleyhayworth@hotmail.com

> **Remuneration**: production, cash prize.

> **Preference.** Length: 10 minutes or less. Material Must Be: unproduced, unpublished.

> **Application**. Submit best play to haleyhayworth@hotmail.com. Deadline: May 1.

Stage Left Theatre
National Contest for the Worst Ten-Minute Play
3408 N. Sheffield Ave., Chicago, IL 60657
John Sanders, Director of New Play Development
773-883-8830 ext.3
drekfest@stagelefttheatre.com
www.stagelefttheatre.com

> **Consideration.** Fee: $10 (goes towards the cash prize). Remuneration: $100.

> **Preference.** Length: 10-minutes.

> **Application.** See website. Mail your submissions to: Stage Left Theatre, 3408 N. Sheffield Ave., Chicago, IL 60657, ATTN: DrekFest. Or email drekfest@stagelefttheatre.com. Deadline: May 1, 2007.

FUSION Theatre
Ten Minute New Play Festival
700 1st Street NW, Albuquerque, New Mexico 87102
jeng@fusionabq.org
www.fusionabq.org

> **Consideration:** production, award. Fees: $5. Disclosure: offset printing costs, Remuneration: jury prize.

> **Preference.** Length: 10 pages or less, Content/Subject Matter: see website. Material Must Be: unproduced, not previously submitted.

> **Application.** Play with title page and contact info, fee with e-submission at: http://thecell.fatcow.com/store/page6.html, or mail to: FUSION Theatre Co., Attn: Jen Grigg, 700 1st Street NW, Albuquerque, New Mexico 87102. Deadline: May, exact deadline and theme announced in February, check website.

The Westcliffe Center for the Performing Arts
New Rocky Mountain Voices Competition
Steve Miller, New Rocky Mountain Voices Program Coordinator
719-783-9344
smiller012@centurytel.net
http://www.jonestheater.com/NRMV-2008.htm

> **Consideration.** Fees: $5 for each play submitted (make check out to "WCPA").

> **Preference.** Length: not exceed 30 minutes. 6 or fewer actors. Author Must Be: currently residing in or attending an educational institution in Arizona, Colorado, or New Mexico.. Material Must Be: unpublished.

> **Application.** Send four copies of the manuscript with no mention of the author's name or contact information anywhere in the manuscript, fee, cover letter to include a summary of the author's theater and playwriting experience and goals, mailing address, email address, telephone number and other pertinent contact information. Send to: New Rocky Mountain Voices, C/O Custer County Library, PO Box 689, Westcliffe, CO, 81252 (for United States Postal Service); or New Rocky Mountain Voices, C/O Custer County Library, 209 Main Street, Westcliffe, CO, 81252 (for UPS or FEDEX). Deadline: May 1, 2008 (postmark).

Chameleon Theatre Circle's Annual New Play Contest
The Chameleon Theatre Circle
16795 Hershey Court, Lakeville, MN 55044
chameleon@seetheatre.org
www.chameleontheatre.org
http://www.seetheatre.org/newplay/NPC9-EntryForm.pdf

> **Consideration.** Remuneration: 3-5 Winners will receive $25, reading.

> **Preference.** Length: 15 pages or less. Material Must Be: unproduced

> **Application.** See website http://www.seetheatre.org/newplay/NPC9-EntryForm.pdf. Submit three (3) copies of each script to 9th Annual New Play Contest, The Chameleon Theatre Circle, 819 E. 145th St.; Burnsville, MN 55337. Do not bind any author identification with your scripts. Include the show's title on at least the first bound page. Deadline: Rolling until May 4, 2009.

The Image Theater
Young Playwrights 10-Minute Play Contest
Ten Minute Play Contest Entry
68 Oakland St., Lowell, MA 01851
978-441-0102
www.imagetheater.com

> **Consideration.** Type of Opportunity: youth award, production. Remuneration: First prize $100 and a full production; Second Prize, $50 and a staged reading; Third Prize: $25 and a staged reading.

> **Preference.** Length: 10 pages. Production: 6 characters or less, simple set. Author Must Be: 14-18 years old and live near Lowell, MA.

> **Application.** Submissions must be bound, with a cover page including your name, address, phone number, and e-mail, if applicable. Submit to: The Image Theater, Ten Minute Play Contest Entry, 68 Oakland Street, Lowell, MA 01851. Deadline: May 25.

The Actors' Theatre
The Actors' Theatre 15th Annual Ten-Minute Play Contest
Actors' Theatre
1001 Center St., Santa Cruz, CA 95060
www.actorssc.org
www.actorssc.org/contests.php#810s

> **Consideration.** Fees: $10 per play.

> **Preference.** Length: 10 pages maximum. Minimal set requirements. Material Must Be: unproduced, unpublished.

Application. Submit 5 copies of your play (securely bound, preferably in a soft cover). Two types of cover pages: 1) a separate cover letter, which includes your name, address, phone number, e-mail and the play title. 2) the play title on each copy. No identifying information on the script other than the title. Submission: mail five hard copies (see address above) to TEN-MINUTE PLAY CONTEST. Deadline: June 1.

Circus Theatricals
One Act Play Festival
310-226-6144 ext. 1
info@circustheatricals.com
www.circustheatricals.com
www.circustheatricals.com/playwrights.html

Preference. Length: 15 pages or less, simple production value.

Application. Submit three copies of full script, typed and securely bound. No contact info on script/separate title page with contact info. Short bio. Previous production history. Submit to: Circus Theatricals, Attn: One Act Plays Festival 2008, PO Box 586 Culver City , CA 90232. Deadline: June 30, 2008.

Women At Play(s)
At Play(s) 4
mariannesawchuk@hotmail.com
www.womenatplays.com

Consideration. Remuneration: depends on box office.

Preference. Length: 20 minutes or less. Content/Subject Matter: All characters must be female. Author Must Be: female. Material Must Be: unproduced and unpublished.

Application. Submit play with contact info to: mariannesawchuk@ hotmail.com. Deadline: June 30.

Future Tenant
Future 10
Stacey Vespaziani
Future 10 Play Submissions
3251 Pinehurst Ave., Pittsburgh, PA 15216
svespaz@mac.com
http://www.futuretenant.org/programs_FutureTen.html

Consideration. Production.

Preference. Length: approx 10 pages. Theme: "Life in Pittsburgh." Production: Cast size 2-6, limited set/prop requirements.

Application. Submit four copies of play, plus a cover letter with all contact info and title of play. No contact info or name should be on submitted scripts. Deadline: July 15.

UMBC Department of Theatre
IN10 National Play Competition
1000 Hilltop Circle, Baltimore, MD 21250
http://www.umbc.edu/theatre/In10.html

Remuneration: $1,000 prize and a staged reading.

Preference. Length: 10 minutes. Content/Subject Matter: plays written for female characters age 16 to 30.

Application: See website. Submit play and application to: Professor Susan McCully, 10-Minute Play Competition, UMBC Department of Theatre, 1000 Hilltop Circle, Baltimore, MD 21250. Deadline: September 1st.

Six Women Play Festival
c/o Pikes Peak Arts Council
PO Box 1073, Colorado Springs, CO 80901
www.sixwomenplayfestival.com
http://www.sixwomenplayfestival.com/guidelines.html

Remuneration: $100 and a travel stipend to attend the festival.

Preference. Length: 10 pages. Content/Subject Matter: theme of "changes and transitions." Author Must Be: female. Material Must Be: unpublished, unproduced.

Application: Submit three copies of play (bound with staple only) with title only. Include one unbound sheet which includes title of play, author's name and address, email, and phone number. Submission period: September 1 -December 31.

Theatre Three
Festival of One-Act Plays
P.O. Box 512, Port Jefferson, NY 11777-0512
www.theatrethree.com
http://www.theatrethree.com/oneactsubmissionguidelines.htm

Consideration. Remuneration: small stipend, production.

Preference. Length: 40 minutes maximum. Simple set, 8 actors or less. Material Must Be: unproduced, no adaptations, musicals, or children's plays.

Application. Submit a cover letter, a synopsis, and a resume along with one copy of the play. Cover sheet of play should have title, author, author's address, author's telephone number, and author's email address (if available). Plays should be neatly bound or stapled on the left-hand corner. (No loose pages and no binders, please.) All submissions must include a standard SASE for correspondence. Submit to The 13th Annual Festival of One-Act Plays, Attn: Jeffrey Sanzel, Artistic Director, THEATRE THREE, P.O. Box 512, Port Jefferson, NY 11777-0512. Deadline: September 30 (postmark).

Potluck Productions
Kansas City Women's Playwriting Festival
7338 Belleview, Kansas City, MO 64114
www.kcpotluckproductions.com

Consideration. Remuneration: production.

Preference. Length: 10-20 minutes. Author Must Be: female. Material Must Be: unpublished.

Application. Send two (2) paper copies of your script (bound), a show synopsis, resume, and cover letter. Enclose two (2) SASE envelopes or postcards. Submit to: Potluck Productions, 7338 Belleview, Kansas City, MO 64114. Deadline: Oct. 1 2008. http://www.kcpotluckproductions. com/script_submissions.htm

StageQ
Queer Shorts, c/o StageQ
PO Box 8876, Madison, WI. 53708-8876
www.stageq.com

Preference. Length: 5-15 minutes. Content/Subject Matter: queer lifestyle.

Application. Email play, paragraph synopsis, production requirements, cast breakdown, and if there are any queer characters or nudity to QueerShorts@stageq.com, or mail to: Queer Shorts, c/o StageQ, PO Box 8876, Madison, WI. 53708-8876. Deadline: October, check website for details.

Camino Real Playhouse
ShowOff Playwriting Festival
Tom Scott, Director
Playwriting Contest
31776 El Camino Real, San Juan Capistrano, CA 92675
949-248-0808
info@city-theater.org, pantheater@comcast.net
http://www.caminorealplayhouse.org/ShowOffs.html

> **Consideration:** Contest, production. Fees: A $10.00 per play. Disclosure: for use as winner stipends. Remuneration: not specified.
>
> **Preference.** Length: 10 minutes.
>
> **Application.** Submit plays unbound (stapled is OK) with your full contact info on the cover or title page to: ShowOff!, Camino Real Playhouse, 31776 El Camino Real, San Juan Capistrano, CA 92675. Deadline: October 15th each year.

West Coast Ten Minute Play Contest and Festival
Jill Forbath, Artistic Director
West Coast Ten-Minute Play Contest
P.O. Box 18438, Irvine, CA 92623-8438
http://www.calactors.com/upnt.htm

> **Remuneration:** The first, second, and third place winners will receive $100, $75, and $50 respectively, and performances in the Annual West Coast Ten-Minute Play Festival "Six At Eight". The fourth place winning play will receive performances in the opening and closing.
>
> **Preference.** Two entries maximum per playwright; contest open to playwrights living in the USA. Length: ten pages only. Content/Subject Matter: no musicals, one-acts, or children's plays; no plays previously given an equity performance.
>
> **Application.** No electronic submissions; "snail mail" only. Please, no Express Mail! Deadline is November 1st of every year.

Lakeshore Players
Ten-Minute Play Contest
Outreach Committee
4820 Stewart Ave., White Bear Lake, MN 55110
www.lakeshoreplayers.com

> **Remuneration:** production, $10 per performance.
>
> **Preference.** Length: 10 minutes. Production: 5 or fewer characters.

Application. Submit two copies of script (One with contact information, one with title only) to: Lakeshore Players Outreach Committee, 4820 Stewart Ave. White Bear Lake, MN   55110. Deadline: November, check website for details.

Actors Theatre of Louisville
National Ten-Minute Play Contest
316 West Main S., Louisville, KY 40202-4218
www.actorstheatre.org
http://actorstheatre.org/humana_contest.htm

Consideration. Remuneration: $1000, production.

Preference. Length: 10 pages or less. Author Must Be: US citizen. Material Must Be: unproduced, not previously submitted.

Application. Submit play with contact info to: National Ten-Minute Play Contest, Actors Theatre of Louisville, 316 West Main Street, Louisville, KY 40202-4218. Deadline: November 2009, check website for details.

Moving Arts
Premiere One-Act Competition
www.movingarts.org/submission_guidelines.html

Consideration. $10 entry fee per script (made out to Moving Arts). Remuneration: $200.

Preferences: One-Acts.

Application. Submit script, cover letter, SASE to Moving Arts, Premiere One-Act Competition, P.O. BOX 481145, Los Angeles, CA 90048. Playwright's name should appear only on the cover letter and nowhere on the script. Scripts must be three-hole punched, preferably with a cover–please do not send loose sheets or spiral bound scripts. Deadline: November 1 - January 31 (postmark).

Over Our Head Players
Snowdance 10 Minute Comedy Festival
SNOWDANC
c/o Sixth Street Theatre
318 6th St., Racine, WI, 53403
www.overourheadplayers.org

Consideration. production, prize. Remuneration: A cash award of $300, $100 to second and third place.

Preference. Length: 10 minutes. Content/Subject Matter: comedy. Material Must Be: unpublished.

Application. Submit play with contact info to: SNOWDANC, c/o Sixth Street Theatre, 318 6th St.,Racine, WI, 53403. Deadline: November, check website for details.

Source Festival

1835 14th St., NW, Washington, DC 20009

202-315-1305

www.sourcedc.org

www.sourcedc.org/sourcefestival/html/10minute.html

www.sourcedc.org/sourcefestival/html/submissions.html

Consideration. Remuneration: production.

Preference. Length: 10 minutes. Material Must Be: unpublished.

Application. Submit play with contact info on title page and submission form on website. Plays only accepted in following formats: .doc, .pdf, or .rtf. All pages must have number and include title of play and name of playwright. One submission per applicant. Deadline: November, check website for details.

Gallery Players' Annual Black Box
New Play Festival

The Gallery Players

Attn: Black Box

199 14th St., Brooklyn, NY 11215

www.galleryplayers.com

Consideration. Production

Preference. Length: 10-60 minutes Content/Subject Matter: Seeking all subjects and styles. Material Must Be: unproduced.

Application. For more information, guidelines and a downloadable application form please. No e-mail submissions accepted. Deadline: December 1.

Rolling or Ongoing Deadlines

Atlantis Playmakers
SAS PlayFEST
4611 Monroe St., Hollywood FL, 33021
www.atlantisplaymakers.com

> **Consideration:** reading/production. **Remuneration:** award.
>
> **Preference.** Length: 15 minutes or less. Production: 2-5 actors, simple set. Content/Subject Matter: theme-based, see website. Material Must Be: unproduced.
>
> **Application.** Submit to 4611 Monroe St., Hollywood FL, 33021, or email Word format **ONLY** to kdb@AtlantisPlaymakers.com. Entries must include a cover page with the playwright's name, address, phone, and e-mail. Deadline: rolling, see website

Chicago Dramatists
1005 W. Chicago Ave., Chicago, IL 60622
312-633-0630
http://www.chicagodramatists.org/playwrights/#1071404052191349

> **Consideration.** Full workshop (rehearsal, performance, discussion)
>
> **Preference.** Length: Submissions must be ten pages or less, standard 12-pt. font size, pages numbered, contain no more than six characters, and will not be returned. Content/Subject Matter: No musicals; binding, staples, faxes, or e-mailed submissions. Playwrights may submit no more than one piece to each workshop.
>
> **Application.** Playwrights must include their day and evening phone numbers and a character list with ages. Submission rules and deadlines are announced in the theatre's quarterly flyers and on its web site. Unsolicited scripts for 10-Minute Workshop must be preceded by a phone call requesting guidelines.

Chatham Playhouse
Annual Jersey Voices Festival
973-635-7363
jerseyvoices@chathamplayers.org
www.chathamplayers.org/jerseyvoices.html

> **Preference.** Length: 20 minute or less. Author Must Be: New Jersey playwright.

Application. Submit play to Jersey Voices c/o CCP, P.O. Box 234, Chatham, NJ 07928 or email (in Word of PDF format) to jerseyvoices@ chathamplayers.org. **Deadline:** rolling

li'l sticky, the 10-minute bar play series
Blue Box Productions
blueboxworld@gmail.com
http://web.mac.com/blueboxworld/iWeb/Site/Send%20us%20things.html

Consideration. Remuneration: production.

Preference. Length: no more than 10 pages. Content/Subject Matter: plays must be set in a bar, 4 characters or fewer.

Application. Each play must have: a title page with title, writer's name(s) and contact information, production history and page numbers must be on each page. Plays must be in pdf, final draft or word format. Submit to: blueboxworld@gmail.com, with subject line ' Li'l Sticky 10-minute play submission.' **Deadline:** rolling.

Live Girls! Theater
Ongoing. Quickies - the annual festival of shorts
www.livegirlstheater.org

Consideration: production or reading.

Preferences. Small cast and low production requirements. Length: 10-minute. Author Must Be: Female.

Application. Email plays and include your bio\resume, production history for plays submitted to: submissions@livegirlstheater.org. Attach plays as Word docs. **Deadline:** ongoing.

Pan Theater
Pan Theater Play Festival
287 17th Street, #220, Oakland, CA 94612
www.pantheater.com

Consideration. Production.

Preference. Length: 10 minutes or less. Content/Subject Matter: Shorter plays/blackouts are good. Comedy and absurdity are good, but we also choose more dramatic pieces. Please review the notes for submission guidelines. Production date is September.

Application. There is a two play limit per author/per a category. Send two copies of each play with the second copy marked reading copy. We are no longer accepting electronic submissions! No materials are returned/ we do not send out notification emails. Winners titles/authors are posted to the Web site. What to include: Writer's info, Production/ Reading History, Synopsis/Character Info, Production suggestions, Full contact information. Deadlines: ongoing.

The Poco Loco Players
pocolocoplayers@yahoo.com

Consideration. Production.

Preference. Interested in scripts set in New Mexico or written by New Mexican authors, and also scripts written by young people or written for young actors, but they're willing to consider any short play. Length: 1-10 minutes long. Content/Subject Matter: Scripts must use simple sets & props, and have small casts (1-3 preferred).

Application. Email. Ongoing deadline.

Sundog Theatre
Scenes from the Staten Island Ferry
718-816-5453
info@sundogtheatre.org
www.sundogtheatre.org

Consideration: prize, production. Remuneration: $100.

Preference. Length: 10 minutes. Content/Subject Matter: would take place on the Staten Island Ferry

Application. Submit script to info@sundogtheatre.org. Deadline: rolling.

TheatreRats
Chester Horn Short Play Festival
www.theatrerats.com

Consideration. Remuneration: production.

Preference. Length: no more than 15 pages

Application. Submit script (PDF or Word) to scripts@theatrerats. com. Deadline: rolling.

See Websites for Deadlines

Beyond The Proscenium Productions' Annual Summer Shorts

www.beyondtheproscenium.org

Consideration. Production.

Preference. Guidelines: edgy, bold plays. Length: 5 to 20 pages, should involve no more than six actors and should have minimal set requirements. Content/Subject Matter: Edgy, bold short plays that push the boundaries of theatre in terms of text, movement, and design. Non-linear and untraditional storytelling is desired. Please, no kitchen-sink dramas, musicals, or romantic stories. We are a progressive theatre company looking for work that re-defines the future of theatrical performance.

Application. Playwrights may send their scripts via email or regular mail (be sure to include a self-addressed envelope with the proper postage if you wish the scripts returned)

Brown Couch Theatre Company 10-Minute Play Festival

www.browncouchtheatre.org

Consideration. Production

Preference. Length: Ten minute plays. Content/Subject Matter: Each year is a specific theme.

Application. Please include a title page and a character breakdown at the beginning of your script. Your name should only appear on the title page. Your name will not be released to the reading committee, to ensure objectivity. Scripts may only be submitted electronically. We understand that this may leave some people out, but our entire reading and selection process is done online, and we can't make exceptions. Please send all scripts as an attachment to plays@browncouchtheatre.org.

City Playhouse
Short Play Festival

c/o LACC Theatre Academy

855 N. Vermont Ave., Los Angeles, CA 90029

http://theatreacademy.lacitycollege.edu/theatre/shrtply.htm

City Playhouse sponsors the Short Play Festival. Scripts selected receive a fully mounted production by City Playhouse, in association with the Theatre Academy, as a part of the regular season. Winners work with theatre professionals, including actors, designers, and directors.

Located about a mile from the Paramount Studios lot in Hollywood, the City Playhouse has produced, among others; *After the Fall, The Kentucky Cycle, The Grapes of Wrath, Our Country's Good, The Rose Tattoo,* and the Short Play Festival. The City Playhouse has created an ongoing relationship with many professionals in the film industry and in theatres including the Odyssey, A Noise Within, the CAST, the Colony, the Company of Angels, East LA Classic Theatre, and Shakespeare Festival/ LA.

The purpose of the Short Play Festival is to support new plays and showcase Theatre Academy students and professionals to the Hollywood community. There is currently no other regularly produced Festival on a Los Angeles university or college campus which presents such a wide variety of writers in a single event.

E.S.T. In Aspen, HBO Comedy Arts Festival
Risa Bramon Garcia & Debra Stricklin, Executive Producers
2049 Century Park East, 42nd Fl., Los Angeles, CA 90067
310-201-9575
submissions@hbocomedyfestival.com
http://www.hbocomedyfestival.com/

Consideration. Production

Preference. Comedies. Length: 10-40 minutes long.

Application. Send three copies of each play. Limit three plays.

Full Circle Theatre Company
42 Wayne St. Suite #3, Jersey City, NJ 07302
201-395-9035

Consideration. Production

Preference. Length: Must read no longer than 12 minutes. We produce 6 scripts. Content/Subject Matter: The set must be relatively black box. It will have to be taken down/put up within just a few minutes (if that).

Gardner-Webb University's
New Plays Festival
Scot Lahaie, Director of Theater
Gardner-Webb University
Campus Box 7273, Boiling Springs, NC 28017
www.theater.gardner-webb.edu

Consideration. Production.

Preference. Length: short one-acts and 10 minute plays. Content/Subject Matter: Cast size is unimportant. Unit set or single location is required. No nudity or onstage sex. No film scripts for adaptation. Material Must Be: unproduced and unpublished.

Application. Send scripts electronically (preferred) to Professor Scot Lahaie at slahaie@gardner-webb.edu

Generic Theater's 10 Minute Play Festival

Generic Theater
Box 11071, Norfolk, VA 23517
www.generictheater.org

Preference. Length: Scripts should be approximately 7-10 pages typed in 12 point font on 8.5"x11" paper in standard play script format, and must have a reading time of no more than 10 minutes. Content/Subject Matter: We are looking for fun, dramatic, quirky, inspirational, comic, thought-provoking, you name it, pieces! Minimal to no set. Set should be able to be suggested. No more than 4 characters. Scripts should be a complete play, not an excerpt from a longer work. Plays must be original works that have never had a production. Prior staged readings and amateur/college productions are permissible.

Application. One cover letter. The cover letter should contain the following information: the title of the piece, your name, address and full contact information, one paragraph synopsis of your piece, one paragraph biography. Scripts cannot be submitted by e-mail. More than one script may be submitted.

Herring Run Theater Artsfest

B. Catalano, Artistic Director
70 Cape Drive 1B, Mashpee, MA 02649
508-423-2994
bcatalano@mail.capecod.com
www.herringrunartsfest.org

Consideration. Production. 12 scripts, and presenting 6 plays over 2 weekend evenings in September.

Preference. Length: No more than 12 minutes each. Content/Subject Matter: We encourage innovative and fresh style, all subjects.

Application. While we select from all states, preference is given to writers from the Northeast. No payment to writer.

Howling Moon Cab Company's
Brooklyn Plays Festival

Consideration. Production

Preference. Length: 10 minute plays, no more than 12 pages. Content/ Subject Matter: Brooklyn stories, reflecting both the mythos and the reality of the borough. We are looking for works which take place in Brooklyn's very diverse communities, and which most of all have some reason to take place there; plays which tell us something about Brooklyn, and in which the events are partly determined by the setting. Minimal sets and no more than five actors.

Application. Email your work as a MS Word (preferred) or .pdf file attachment to Jonathan Wallace at jw@bway.net

The Kennedy Center's American College Theatre Festival
Address varies depending on your region of the country
http://kennedy-center.org/education/actf/

Consideration. Eligibility for entering a 10-minute play in the national showcase is based on whether the playwright's school has entered a participating or associate level entry in KC/ACTF during the festival year. Plays from schools that do not have a participating or associate entry will submit a $20 fee for each 10-minute play payable to the region. The 10-minute play competition is limited to students enrolled in a college or university during the festival year.

Preference. Length: There is a 10-minute (7-10 pages, 12 point font) limit for each play.

Application. A first-place award of $1000 will be given to the playwright selected from the national festival finalists. Selection of the national winner is based on a reading of the 8 finalists plays by the national selection team. For more information on entering a 10-minute play, contact the New Plays Program chair in your region of the country. If you're unfamiliar with who this person is, visit the KC/ACTF website.

New York Collective For The Arts'
Annual 10-Minute Play Festival
NY Collective Theatre
315 Bleecker St. No. 313, New York, New York 10014
tenminutes@nycollective.org

Consideration. Production

Preference. Length: All plays should run a maximum of ten minutes. Plays longer than ten minutes will not be considered. ONE play entry per playwright. Additional plays will not be considered. Content/Subject Matter: All plays MUST have between 2 and 4 characters. Plays with more than 4 characters will not be considered. Material Must Be: unproduced and unpublished. Plays that have already received an Equity production will NOT be considered.

Application. Your submission must include a title page: name, address, e-mail, and phone number. Submissions MUST be received via e-mail or be *in hand* by deadline date. Entries will be acknowledged by e-mail reply only. Winners will be notified in April. Due to the volume of scripts submitted we cannot provide feedback on individual work.

CHAPTER 7

Shut Up and Show Me

Trying to decide how to share examples of ten-minute plays with you has been a big, splittin' headache. Do I give you what I think are seven of the best plays I can find? Do I show you plays that are good but have all kind of structural problems so that we can have a hot discussion of their strengths and weaknesses? Do I compare one to the other, or make no comparisons at all and let you draw the comparisons? Should I share a play with you that's too early in its development to really be appreciated, but has a terrific germ of an idea that just needs further exploring? What would be most helpful?

What stumped me for the longest time was that I can't be sitting across a table from you, helping you decipher what you may or may not understand. I can't be there to hear you laugh, or throw this book down when you get confused or even bored with one of the plays. And I can't give you a writing aesthetic that contends that "this is good, and this is not" without understanding more of your own sensibility. So what I'm going to do is ask you questions about the plays and let you make your own discoveries of their complexity.

I chose the plays for this book because I've seen them in production and I know the writing is successful on many levels. After all, a play is dramatic literature until it hits the stage and makes a theatrical transformation. I also chose the plays knowing that the stories in each play are *character-driven* and not *plot-driven*; very little happens, story-wise, in the course of each play. The dramatic arc of each story is propelled by character discoveries and transformations and not plot points that heighten dramatic action. As I've said many times across all my years of teaching, you will never write a story more interesting than the characters (or people) in the story. It's impossible. People are outrageously complex and are made more so when a need, want or desire is heightened for very human reasons.

Chances are you're not going to like all seven plays, but I assure you there's something important to learn from each play if you study the craft involved with creating very different worlds peopled by emotionally knotted human beings. Discover for yourself what tools each playwright uses to tell a simple story: intent, dramatic structure, metaphor, dialogue, mystery and theatricalism. Search for the honesty in the writing – those moments you sense the dramatist has connected to some universal truth that is revealed through a thoughtful understanding of a complicated life. David Crespy, a playwright featured in the first edition of this book, spoke to such honesty when he offered, "I just think it's part of the job of the dramatist to write from the heart, and put oneself at risk in the writing of a play. If a play doesn't cost you something to write, then maybe it's not really worth the effort…Bottom line, to write a play is to reveal myself as a human being; that's your job as a writer. We owe our audiences a play that is terrifying for us to write and forces us to take risks."

Read the work, take notes and answer the questions that follow each play. I've given you questions to think about in the first five plays; form your own questions for the last two. I guarantee you'll learn something.

This Really Cool Guy I Met at The Mall

By Matthew Rasenick

Characters:

     JAMES

     TARA

Time: Today

Setting: A suburban mall

> *Lights up. On the stage is a small table with chairs on either side and a man in his mid-twenties, head to toe in logo-wear. He sits with a tray of fast food on the table. He has a cell phone to his ear.*

JAMES: Yeah, I'm just hangin' here ... At the food court. ...Yeah, you know, scouting the prospects ... Right ... Right ... Naw ...

A fourteen-year-old girl enters stage left, dressed like a fourteen-year-old girl. She walks by James, carrying a tray of Taco Bell. He watches her.

JAMES: Yo, hold up.

He tilts away his phone and calls out to the girl.

JAMES: Hey. Come over here, girl.

She turns around and smiles.

JAMES: Com'ere for a sec.

She looks the other way to check to see if he's talking to someone else.

JAMES: Yeah, it's you...

She smiles again and stands still, looking back briefly, then to him again.

JAMES: Come over here and say hi. You were just gonna walk right by me, weren't you.

She keeps smiling but doesn't move.

JAMES: What're you doin'? I ain't gonna bite you. Sit down for a sec.

She moves a little closer. He closes his phone and puts it in his pocket.

JAMES: *(Gently.)* What's your name?

TARA: *(Embarrassed.)* Tara [tar-uh].

JAMES: Tara [tear-uh]?

She nods coyly.

JAMES: My name's James.

He sticks out his hand and she shakes it, moving a little closer.

TARA: Hi.

JAMES: I saw you here last week, didn't I?

She nods again.

JAMES: So we know each other.

She shrugs.

JAMES: So you got no reason to be afraid of me, right? *(smiles)* What'd you get at Taco Bell?

TARA: A chicken soft taco.

JAMES: That's all? Just one taco? You're not real hungry.

She shakes her head no.

JAMES: Can you do me a favor, Tara?

TARA: What kind of favor?

JAMES: Just sit down for a second. 'Cause I was waiting for a friend of mine here, he just called and told me he can't make it. You think you can give me some company for a minute?

TARA: My friends are over there.

JAMES: They'll be alright without you for a minute, don't you think?

She shrugs. He gets up and goes around her to the other side of the table, pulling out her chair. She lets him take her tray from her and put it down on the table. Then he waits with his hands on the back of the chair, for a second, until she sits.

JAMES: There you go. *(sits back down on his side of the table)* So, Tara [tear-uh]?

She first nods, then:

TARA: *(Correcting his pronunciation.)* TAHR-uh.

JAMES: TAHR-uh? Oh, I'm sorry, was I saying it wrong? I'm sorry, you should have said something.

TARA: That's okay.

JAMES: What you doing at the mall today?

TARA: Just hanging out. With my friends.

JAMES: You buy anything?

TARA: Some CDs.

JAMES: Yeah, what'd you get?

TARA: Sum 41 and Justin Timberlake.

JAMES: You like JT? That's my boy. I was in LA two weeks ago, gave him a call, we hung out. He's a real cool guy. *(She's smiling.)* Oh what, you don't believe me? Oh, no, I understand. You think I'm misrepresenting myself here, yeah, no, I know a lot of those guys, so it's not a big deal to me, so you know I never think people wouldn't believe me. But that's okay, I wasn't trying to impress you or anything, I was just telling it 'cause you mentioned his name. That's cool though. *(Nods for a second.)* You like him though? You like that?

TARA: That's why I got the CD.

JAMES: *(Laughs.)* Yeah, I guess it is. Right? *(Takes a sip of his soda)* You should feel free to eat your food at any time. Open up that taco before it gets cold, right?

> She opens her taco and takes a bite.

JAMES: So you buying some CDs, that's cool. I was thinking about maybe stopping by Musicland ... *(Points offstage right, toward the audience.)* ... maybe later. I don't know. Any CDs you think are good, I should check out? *(She pauses.)* I already got my man JT's last one, but I don't think I know that other one you said. What was that?

TARA: Sum 41.

JAMES: Yeah, Sum 41, I should get that you think? That's good?

TARA: They're one of my favorite bands.

JAMES: Really? I'll have to look at that. I've heard people, you know, like a lot of my friends been talking about that but I haven't got around to buying it.

TARA: I like them and Good Charlotte. And Blink 182.

JAMES: Sum 42 and Blink 182. You like the ones with the numbers, is that right?

TARA: I guess so.

JAMES: You buy a lot of CDs?

TARA: When I have money.

JAMES: Yeah, I remember when I was your age, a few years ago, I always wished I had more money 'cause there was a lot of stuff I wanted, right? Is it that way for you?

TARA: CDs are too expensive.

JAMES: Yeah, but what can you do, right? You gotta have CDs, you gotta have the clothes you want ... All that. (*She waits a second, then takes another bite of her taco.*) So you probably come here a lot, right? On the weekend especially, right? You in school? Where you go to school?

TARA: D...

JAMES: Wait, no, don't tell me, I bet I can guess. I bet five dollars I'll bet you I can guess. Alright? Five dollars, you go to the University offfff ... (*She smiles, knowingly.*) No? I'm wrong? What, where you go? Are you still in high school?

TARA: I'm only a sophomore.

JAMES: You're a sophomore? In high school? You look a lot older, I wouldn't ever think that. You knew I was gonna say that though, didn't you. You tricked me on purpose.

TARA: (*Smile busting open.*) No.

> He takes a wallet out of his back pocket, pulls a five dollar bill and puts it on her tray.

JAMES: You sure you're not in college?

TARA: I'm sure.

JAMES: I thought you were for sure. I thought I'd seen you around.

TARA: You're not in college.

JAMES: What's that supposed to mean. You think I look stupid? I go to college. You ever heard of Northwestern?

TARA: You go to Northwestern?

JAMES: Yeah, it's right by here; it's like ten minutes that way.

TARA: I know that.

JAMES: Why, you think I look too young?

TARA: My cousin goes there.

JAMES: Yeah, what's his name?

TARA: She's a girl.

JAMES: What's her name?

> *A cutesy ring-tone goes off. Tara takes her phone out of her pocket and puts it to her ear.*

TARA: Hello?... Yeah, I'm over here. *(Waves offstage right.)* Why?... Okay, not now... No ... Why are you being like that?... Okay... Yeah, okay.

> *She pushes a button and puts the phone in her pocket. She's about to say something but he does first.*

JAMES: What's your cousin's name?

TARA: Jenna.

JAMES: Yeah, I know a girl named Jenna.

TARA: *(Thinks.)* Does she have ... blonde hair?

JAMES: Yeah, Jenna. blonde hair... she's real pretty...

TARA: No, Jenna has brown hair.

She looks serious, then smiles.

JAMES: Oh, I see, you said that to try and trick me. (*Smiles and throws a french fry at her, playfully, or maybe a little harder than that. She laughs.*) Well then I guess I don't know her, 'cause the Jenna I know... (*Throws another fry at her, not as hard.*)...has blonde hair. It's a different one I bet though, right? It's a big college so I bet there's probably like ten girls there with the same name.

TARA: What year are you?

JAMES: What year?

TARA: Like are you a freshman, sophomore, junior, or senior?

JAMES: Junior.

TARA: Oh. She's a freshman.

JAMES: Yeah, I guess she's not the one I know. I bet she's a cool girl though; there's a lot of cool girls there. It's a pretty cool place. You should come there.

TARA: I don't think I could get in.

JAMES: No, I bet you could. I'm real good at reading people when I meet them, you know? And I can tell you're a smart girl.

TARA: I don't get good grades.

JAMES: I think you can get good grades if you try hard enough. Do you try pretty hard?

TARA: Not as hard as I can, but...

JAMES: You need to try as hard as you can if you want to be as good as you can be, right? I think you can do whatever you wanna do. What do you wanna do?

TARA: I wanna be a doctor.

JAMES: Really? That's pretty cool.

TARA: What are you gonna do?

JAMES: I don't know. I got some different things I do, you know? But I think I wanna be maybe like a singer or something like that, you know?

TARA: Can you sing?

JAMES: *(In fake embarrassment.)* Yeah, a little bit, you know. I don't wanna brag.

TARA: Sing something.

JAMES: I can't do it here. I'm probably gonna do like a concert or something in, like, a couple weeks, you can come see me there if you want.

TARA: Really?

JAMES: Yeah, how 'bout I send you an email?

TARA: Cool, do you have a pen?

> *He pulls a pen out of his pocket and rips a piece of paper from the placemat. He gives them both to her. She writes.*

TARA: That's my IM.

JAMES: Cool. We can hang out. You like to party, Tara?

TARA: *(Smiling.)* Yeah.

JAMES: I bet you do.

TARA: I should go back to my friends though. I said I...

JAMES: Okay, but listen, that was real nice of you to sit and talk to me and I want to thank you.

TARA: That's okay.

JAMES: What's your favorite store here?

TARA: Mavi.

JAMES: What kind of store is that?

TARA: Like cool jeans and clothes and stuff.

JAMES: I'll buy you a present, whatever you want.

TARA: Really?

JAMES: Yeah, pick something. Whatever you want. It'll just take a minute. Call your friends if you want, or I'll tell 'em. Or I think just make 'em wait so they'll be even more jealous when you tell them.

TARA: *(Mischievously.)* Okay.

JAMES: You wanna take the rest of your taco with?

TARA: I don't want any more.

JAMES: You sure?

TARA: Yeah.

> *He puts all their stuff on their trays.*

JAMES: I remember when I was your age, I remember I liked hanging out with kids a few years older, you know? (*Stands up and holds his tray, sipping from the last of his soda.*) It's like 'cause they can afford stuff better than you can so it's not a big deal to them.

> *She stands up and takes hers as he waits and then they start off toward stage left.*

JAMES: If I introduce you to some friends, there's lots of ways you can make a lot of money real easy. 'Cause I bet you like buying a lot of cool stuff, right?

> *He walks behind her as they exit stage left.*

> *Blackout.*

> *END.*

Reader's Questions

1. In the most simple way of thinking, what is this play really about? What could be perceived as two people talking in a mall is actually a predator/victim story. How, then, does the writer reveal the predator's intentions? What makes it a cautionary tale?

2. We've talked about how each character in a ten-minute play should want something, *need* something, and either get what they want or don't. What do James and Tara want from each other? *Why* do you suppose they want what they want? (Why did Tara sit at the table to begin with?) What obstacles stand in their way of getting what they want?

3. The setup here seems simple: a young man and a young girl (strangers to each other) meet one another in mall, speak and at the end of the play, leave together. We know there isn't a strong story-conflict in the play, but there is a very real emotional thread that generates conflict (and suspense) for the audience. How does the dramatist weave that thread through the play to intensify the suspense?

4. The age of the characters (and other people mentioned in the story) seems to make a significant contribution to the storytelling. Why? If either character were just two or three years older, could this story be told?

Boy Marries Hill

By Lindsay Walker

Characters:

>TAPESH, Early to mid-twenties. Indian American, Hindu. Reasonable, matter-of-fact.
>
>DARSHINI, Early to mid-twenties. Indian American, Hindu. Logical, selfish, matter-of-fact.
>
>PIZZA BOY, Middle aged, emotionally broken, never looks up.

Time:　　Modern day.

Setting:　Inside an apartment in any large American city.

>*AT RISE: Center stage: two folding chairs face each other, angled towards the audience. There is a door standing stage right. Darshini sits: stage left chair, hands folded in lap, staring at door, frozen like a mannequin. Tapesh enters abruptly through door, takes off hat.*

TAPESH: Hello Darshini, I have returned from visiting my mother in India.

DARSHINI: *(Rises as if to embrace him.)* Oh, Tapesh. I love you and I have missed you.

TAPESH: *(Holds up a hand, stopping her in her tracks.)* No kisses, Darshini. I am breaking up with you.

DARSHINI: *(Sits down hard.)* Why?

TAPESH: *(Sits, takes her hand.)* I still love you, Darshini, but something has changed and we can't be together anymore.

DARSHINI: What has changed, Tapesh?

TAPESH: I can't tell you.

DARSHINI: *(Rises. Paces.)* This is terrible news, but you can't break up with me.

TAPESH: Why is that?

DARSHINI: Something has changed and it's not just about us anymore.

TAPESH: What do you mean?

DARSHINI: I'm pregnant.

TAPESH: Am I the father?

DARSHINI: Yes.

TAPESH: Are you sure.

DARSHINI: Pretty sure.

TAPESH: I can accept that answer. But I still can't be with you.

DARSHINI: *(Sits.)* You will have to give me an explanation. I love you too much to be okay with this.

TAPESH: I could tell you but you won't believe me. You'll get angry and there'll be unpleasantness.

DARSHINI: There will be more unpleasantness if you don't tell me.

TAPESH: *(Rises. Paces.)* Ok, I'll tell you. (*Pause.*) I have to marry a hill. I have promised myself to it and the hill has accepted.

DARSHINI: A hill? But why, Tapesh?

TAPESH: Because a goddess appeared to my mother in a dream and told her I had to. It's her hill.

DARSHINI: Your mother's?

TAPESH: No, Lakshmi's, the goddess who cursed her.

DARSHINI: I don't believe your mother. I think she made that story up to keep you for herself.

TAPESH: Well I believe her, Darshini, and you don't understand where I'm coming from.

DARSHINI: Do you love the hill more than me?

TAPESH: No, but I am my mother's son and I must honor her wishes.

DARSHINI: What about your son? (*Rubs belly, but it's too early to tell she's pregnant.*) Don't you feel obligated towards him?

TAPESH: *(Sits.)* So it's a boy?

DARSHINI: Yes.

TAPESH: Isn't it too early to know that?

DARSHINI: Medically speaking, yes.

TAPESH: Then how do you know?

DARSHINI: *(Rises. Paces.)* A goddess appeared to me in a dream and told me it was a boy.

TAPESH: So it could be a girl.

DARSHINI: You don't believe me.

TAPESH: I believe you had a dream, but that's not enough evidence to support your claim.

DARSHINI: You are a hypocrite.

TAPESH: There is evidence to support that I suppose.

DARSHINI: Quit flip-flopping. (*Sits.*) We need to talk about this. You can't leave me.

TAPESH: Of course I can. The question is, will I?

DARSHINI: Are you in love with the hill?

TAPESH: *(Rises. Paces.)* No, but this is a real conflict. I need to think about how to proceed.

DARSHINI: Wouldn't your mother want you to be happy?

TAPESH: Yes, but I think I could be happy with a hill; though not as happy as with you and the baby.

DARSHINI: Well, I am also conflicted.

TAPESH: *(Sits.)* How so?

DARSHINI: I want you to stay but I'm beginning to think you're a moron.

TAPESH: And that you'd be better off without me?

DARSHINI: Exactly.

TAPESH: I see your point.

DARSHINI: So what do we do?

TAPESH: If only there was some sort of sign. Something to show us the answers.

> *They both stare into space for a beat. Pizza boy enters stage right, pretends to ring the bell, makes a "ding-dong" noise. They snap their heads towards the door in unison.*

DARSHINI: I wonder who that is?

TAPESH: *(Crosses to door. Looks through peephole.)* Why, it's the pizza boy who never looks up!

DARSHINI: What a fascinating character.

> *Tapesh opens door. Pizza Boy offers pizza without looking up. Stands just inside doorway and head remains down throughout the scene.*

PIZZA BOY: Here is the pizza you ordered.

TAPESH: We didn't order any pizza.

PIZZA BOY: How bizarre. Nice shoes.

TAPESH: Thank you. Say, maybe you can help us.

PIZZA BOY: I doubt it. I have social anxiety and live with my mother.

TAPESH: Why do you live with your mother?

PIZZA BOY: It's a long, sad story.

TAPESH: We'd love to hear an abbreviated version. Wouldn't we, Darshini?

DARSHINI: Oh yes.

PIZZA BOY: I met a girl… I loved the girl… I lost the girl. (*Pause.*) I was broken.

(*Pause.*) Mom took me in.

TAPESH: That is a sad story.

PIZZA BOY: Yes.

TAPESH: Is life with mom better than being broken and alone?

PIZZA BOY: No, I hate my mother; she was fine when I was a kid, but she hasn't changed and I have.

TAPESH: What happened to the girl if you don't mind my asking?

PIZZA BOY: She is married and has a child. She is still beautiful and I deliver her pizza.

DARSHINI: Did she marry a hill?

TAPESH: We have important decisions to make and what you said will surely inform the outcome.

PIZZA BOY: That's nice, but I don't care. I don't care about anything anymore. *(Exits.)*

TAPESH: Good luck, pizza boy. *(Closes door. Crosses back to center.)*

DARSHINI: Are you convinced you should stay with me now?

TAPESH: I'm certainly leaning that way, but there's still the problem of my mother. And what will I tell the hill? *(Sits.)*

DARSHINI: I forgot to ask earlier, but why do you feel so obligated to your mother?

TAPESH: When I was young she saved us from our father.

DARSHINI: Can you elaborate?

TAPESH: Father was a violent man; we were all scared. Mother killed him and we were happy.

DARSHINI: How did she kill him?

TAPESH: She poisoned his eggs one morning and buried him in the backyard.

DARSHINI: Where in the backyard?

TAPESH: Next to a beautiful hill.

DARSHINI: Interesting, let's come back to that. (*Rises. Paces.*) But first, I'd like to know in what other ways did she help you?

TAPESH: She was a very self-sacrificing woman. She sent me to college here in the States.

DARSHINI: What did she want you to accomplish?

TAPESH: She always said she wanted me to learn medicine, marry a local hill – I mean girl –and come back to be the village doctor.

DARSHINI: You are a doctor, but you haven't gone back to India. Why?

TAPESH: Because I met someone here whom I love.

DARSHINI: That is an answer I am happy to hear.

TAPESH: Good. Your happiness is something that is important to me.

DARSHINI: Thank you. It is important to me too.

TAPESH: You are kind of selfish. I never noticed that before.

DARSHINI: Yes. (*Sits.*) It's because I was an only child. I'm used to having things my way.

TAPESH: That makes sense.

DARSHINI: Now, going back to your father's burial. Did your mother bury him near Lakshmi's hill?

TAPESH: (*Rises. Paces.*) Yes, as a matter of fact. (*Pause.*) It really is a lovely hill.

DARSHINI: Assuming your mother truly is cursed, might that have something to do with it?

TAPESH: There is a rumor that the gods curse people who commit crimes too close to their hills.

DARSHINI: Maybe if she dug up the body, your mother's curse would be removed?

TAPESH: That is a very plausible solution.

DARSHINI: If the curse is removed you don't have to marry a hill and our problems are solved.

TAPESH: Yes, but things are more complicated now. *(Sits.)*

DARSHINI: How so?

TAPESH: Well, I still feel guilty about not moving back. My mother really wants me home. And I do have an obligation to the hill.

DARSHINI: I see your point.

TAPESH: Would you consider moving to India with me?

DARSHINI: No. *(Rises. Paces.)*

TAPESH: Why not?

DARSHINI: Because something has changed and we can't be together anymore.

TAPESHI: What has changed since the beginning of this conversation?

DARSHINI: *(Pause.)* I have.

TAPESHI: I see, and how will your change affect me?

DARSHINI: Very badly, I'm afraid. I don't think I love you anymore.

TAPESH: But what about the baby?

DARSHINI: *(Sits.)* There is no baby.

TAPESH: *(Rises.)* I'm confused.

DARSHINI: I lied about the baby to keep you from dumping me.

TAPESH: That is a very unkind thing to do. I'm not sure I can ever trust you again.

DARSHINI: I understand. I only care about myself anyway.

TAPESH: *(Sits.)* It hurts very much when you dump me, you know.

DARSHINI: Yes, it hurt when you dumped me earlier so I can sympathize with what you're feeling.

TAPESH: Maybe it's for the best. After all there's something I haven't told you. *(Rises.)*

DARSHINI: What?

TAPESH: When you lied about being pregnant, all I could think about was my lovely, innocent hill.

DARSHINI: *(Rises.)* So that's what this has really all been about. You're in love with something else.

TAPESH: Yes, I wasn't able to separate my feelings for the hill from the problem with my mother before. It isn't just my mother's plight I see now. *(Pause.)* It is the lovely green hair, the gorgeous topography, the smooth supple curve, the mountain of spices; it is the hill I love.

> Pause. Both start preparing to leave as if cued. Tapesh helps Darshini put on her coat. Darshini hands him his hat.

DARSHINI: A lot has changed in the last ten minutes.

TAPESH: You're right, Darshini, I feel as though I've been on a journey. *(Pause.)* A journey of the heart. *(Crosses to door. Hand on the handle.)*

DARSHINI: And where will your journey end, Tapesh?

> Remains center stage, adjusting her coat, preparing to leave, etc.

TAPESH: It will end where it must. I'm going back to India to marry the hill. *(Pause.)* The hill that I love.

> Exit. Blackout.

> END.

Reader's Questions

1. The two characters in the play, Darshini and Tapesh, are by the dramatist's description, "Indian-American Hindu." What in the story supports that choice? If that description weren't available to us as an audience, and we were only listening to the play, how would that information reveal itself?

2. What function does the Pizza Boy serve in the play? How does he heighten the dramatic action? How does this relate to what Michael Bigelow Dixon describes as "the kick?"

3. How well do you know Darshini and Tapesh as characters? Are you meant to know them well? Or are you meant to know them only as a dramatic articulation (or realization) of a larger story? What is that story?

4. All central characters in our plays take a journey that brings them emotionally from one place to another by the play's end; there is a sense of "inevitability" as the story progresses. In this play, inevitability is not present. Why? How does that serve the dramatic action? How does that inform character? How does that create the style of the play?

Real Life

By Julia Maldonado

Characters:

        ANA

        JAKE

Time: A summer day

Setting: Outside in El Paso, Texas. *110 degrees in the shade hot.*

> *Everything looks hot - very hot. Jake and Ana feel it. Ana,*
> *a Mexican teenage girl, sips an icy drink. She's dressed*
> *eccentrically with kind of an Apache vibe – feathers in her hair,*
> *jewelry you'd buy in Sante Fe, etc.*
>
> *Jake, in his early twenties, holds his drink to his forehead and*
> *neck to keep himself cool. He's a real Texas boy - belt buckle*
> *and all.*

ANA: Have you ever been to New Mexico?

JAKE: No'm.

ANA: I can't believe that. It's just a few hours away. Last winter vacation, my dad and I went to White Sands. You've never been to White Sands?

JAKE: No'm.

ANA: It's amazing! Big, soft white dunes that roll out forever, and up above you there are more stars than sky.

JAKE: I've seen pi'tures.

ANA: It's really not the same thing. You have to feel the sand between your toes. It's like God took a big bag of powdered sugar from his big God fridge and spilled it all over New Mexico.

> *A beat.*

JAKE: Why does God keep the sugar in the fridge?

ANA: Don't you keep the sugar in the fridge?

JAKE: Yes, but God probably don't have to worry about critters.

ANA: Look, it doesn't matter. (*Scoots in close to him.*) How's your smoothie?

JAKE: (*A little uncomfortable.*) It's... it's good. It's cold.

ANA: Which is good. Because it's hot.

JAKE: Uh-huh.

ANA: Hey, James.

JAKE: Jake.

ANA: Jake. I have a question. Why'd you agree to come have smoothies with me? Is it because I'm pretty?

JAKE: (*Startled.*) What? What kinda question is that?

ANA: It's just that I don't get you at all. You don't know me. Why are you smiling? Why are you here? I stole money from your register and the next thing I know, we're having smoothies?

JAKE: You asked me!

ANA: And you said yes!

JAKE: I was being nice.

ANA: Oh, okay. You were being nice. Well that makes all the sense in the world then. If some got me fired, I wouldn't be nice.

JAKE: Oh, I was on the edge of bein' let go anyway. Boss didn't like how I was always... Y'know. Somewhere else.

ANA: Somewhere else?

JAKE: Yeah.

ANA: Where else?

JAKE: I dun' know.

ANA: With a pretty girl somewhere?

JAKE: Anyway, it doesn't matter, because I can just get another job, and it's not a big deal.

ANA: Why get another lame job like that?

JAKE: I need to get paid.

ANA: You know what I do to make money? I sell purses to old ladies that I knit out of plastic bags. Walmart bags are the best because they're that nice blue color. But it's great because I get my materials for free, and then I can sell them at craft sales for a lot of money.

JAKE: That's...

ANA: That's why I came to the Walmart in the first place. Because usually I'm, you know, kind of against Walmart. But I needed more of those bags. It actually isn't really a usual thing for me to, you know. Rob a Walmart. But I didn't really ROB it, I mean, I could have taken ALL your money but I didn't, that would have been wrong. I don't know if you noticed, but I only took like forty bucks. That's nothing. That shouldn't even count as a robbery. I bet you make that much money every time you ring someone up at the Walmart. Besides, who cares if I stole if it's from Walmart? I don't want you to think I'm a bad person just because I tricked you and took Walmart's money.

JAKE: *(Waits for a moment to make sure she's done.)* ... I like to trust in people.

ANA: Well. Good. Because I'm not really a bad person. Unless you want me to be a bad person. Jake, you know what you should do now that you don't have to worry about working at Walmart? Get out of town.

JAKE: I can't.

ANA: Why?

JAKE: My sister.

ANA: What about your sister?

JAKE: Well, she's just about to go to school. I'm helpin' her git there.

ANA: So it's not really that you can't. It's that you don't want to. I doubt you were helping out that much, working at the Walmart. Maybe you could do more for her someplace else.

JAKE: That may be so.

ANA: You know what, it's stupid. You're not obligated to your family anymore. How old are you, James?

JAKE: Jake.

ANA: Jake, how old are you?

JAKE: Twenn'y two.

ANA: See, you're twenty-two. Twenty-two year olds are independent and they don't have to answer to their families or be obligated to them. I'm sixteen, so I have to live with my dad. I have to go to school, even though I don't want to. Classes are lame, and everyone's so dumb and superficial I can't stand it. If I were twenty-two I would get out of here. *(Notices Jake looking at her funny.)* What is it?

JAKE: Oh, you ... you jist talk a lot.

ANA: I bet there's something keeping you here in El Paso. Is it a girlfriend?

JAKE: What? No.

ANA: Well at least I'm not barking up the wrong tree. Not that I would stop barking if you did have a girlfriend. I'm stubborn like that.

JAKE: Um...

ANA: So what is it? What is it that's keeping you here?

JAKE: *(Hesitates.)* Nothin'. I mean, nothin' I can put my finger on. I'm fine here.

ANA: You're just saying that because you've never left. You've never even been to New Mexico. Do you even have a car?

JAKE: I have a truck.

ANA: So go!

JAKE: Well I best not leave if leavin's gonna make me hate my home, you see what I'm sayin'?

ANA: You see, you don't make any sense to me! How could you be happy in this town? With its yellow air and dying grass and this heat, this damn heat... one hundred and ten degrees, one hundred and twenty. We probably shouldn't even be outside because this town is a health hazard.

JAKE: It's alright here.

ANA: If you could just see New Mexico....

JAKE: I reckon you're makin' yourself miserable, bein' so fixed on New Mexico like you are.

ANA: Tell me something about yourself, James. Jake. Anything about you that will help me figure you out. You're happy in El Paso. You agree to have smoothies with a girl who got you fired. You appear to have no wants or desires other than to see your little sister safely off to college. I mean... who are you? Where do you go off to when your boss gets so mad?

JAKE: I– you'll make fun.

ANA: I promise I won't.

JAKE: I like to read comic books. Sometimes I like to think that I'll get home from work and flip on the local news, and find that some feller got struck by lightning or somethin', and suddenly don't answer the call of gravity no more. And he may feel mixed-up and alone, but deep down inside he always knows what the right thing to do is, and in the end, he wins. I like to think about that, but I know that's not real life. Real life is El Paso, and I'm alright with that.

ANA: Real life doesn't have to be El Paso.

JAKE: Well, real life isn't a comic book.

ANA: You may not know why you agreed to have smoothies with me, but I know why I asked you. You could have pinned it all on me and saved your job. But for some reason you didn't. That's not like anything I've seen before.

JAKE: It was my till. My responsibility.

ANA: See. You're different. Say tomorrow your boss got struck by lightning. He probably wouldn't be able to fly. But you? Who knows.

JAKE: *(Blushing.)* Thanks, but I'm not really...

ANA: Do you know what the real difference is between us and people in stories? We dream it, they do it. But you know what? We could do it.

JAKE: We couldn't really.

ANA: No, we could, we could just do it and screw the consequences. Something great happens and you want to dance? You can dance! When someone's bugging you and you just want to scream? You can scream!

JAKE: I guess you could, but–

ANA: I wonder what Ken Clint would do in your situation.

JAKE: Clark Kent.

ANA: I wonder what Clark Kent would do in your situation. Wouldn't he take the beautiful, villainous girl in his arms and give her a kiss that would make her want to put all her evil ways behind her...?

JAKE: No. Clark is happily m–

> *Anna kisses him forcefully. He kisses back, wide-eyed and awkwardly. She breaks the kiss.*

JAKE: ... Um!

> *Jake coughs and clears his throat.*

JAKE: I... There are... *(cough)* Ana, I don't think that was the right thing to do.

ANA: What do you mean?

JAKE: Yer 16!

ANA: So!

JAKE: So there are laws! Seein' as I'm an a-dult. At twen'y-two.

ANA: Oh, we won't get in trouble. Jake, you liked it.

Jake giggles and then nods bashfully.

JAKE: Yeah... yeah it was kinda nice.

Ana tickles him flirtatiously under the chin.

ANA: Jake?

JAKE: Hm?

ANA: Let's go to New Mexico.

JAKE: What?

ANA: Let's go! Let's get in your truck and go! I don't want to go to school, you don't have to go to work, we'll get in the car and drive off into the sunset like in the movies.

JAKE: *(Alarmed.)* Sun doesn't set in the north.

ANA: We'll be going west-ish!

JAKE: Ana... we can't do that.

ANA: Why!

JAKE: What if my truck breaks down?!

ANA: Then we'll continue on into the sunset. On foot. The cold wind will whip sand in our face! Our stomachs will growl with hunger! Yet we will walk, determinedly on, you with your handsome square jaw and me with my strong-yet-delicate figure! We won't stop until we see mountains. 'Til we're in a place where a few months from now we might see snow.

JAKE: I always have wanted to see snow.

ANA: It's the most beautiful thing you could possibly imagine. Not like on TV. It's cold and it hurts your face and makes you squint up your eyes. But when you're in it and it's all around you, it's like for a while you're some place different. Some place decent, some place where people fall down rabbit holes.

JAKE: *(Taking the idea more seriously now, but he's still reluctant.)* But what about your father? What about my sister?

ANA: They aren't really keeping us here.

JAKE: How will we live?

ANA: My purses Jake! There are lots of old hippie ladies in Taos.

JAKE: ... Lots?

ANA: Jake. Nothing's really keeping us from being like the stories.

JAKE: Um. Well.

> *He awkwardly positions himself to kiss her. He's not really sure where to put his hands, and nervously fidgets with his hair and belt buckle.*

JAKE: We could give it a try.

> *He kisses her. Super awkward kiss at first, but as it continues, it gets more intimate and the participants are more elegant and at ease.*

ANA: *(whispers)* Let's go to New Mexico, Jake.

JAKE: *(whispers)* Yeah. Well... Alright.

ANA: We can do whatever we want to do.

JAKE: We can do whatever we want to do. *(Realizing with surprise that it's really true.)* We can do whatever we want to do, Ana! *(firmly)* We can do whatever we want. Anytime. *(Pauses. Urgently.)* Ana?

ANA: What?

JAKE: *(Gravely.)* Without a doubt that's the scariest thing I've ever known.

> *Blackout.*

> *End.*

Reader's Questions

1. All central characters in our plays take a journey that brings them emotionally from one place to another by the play's end. Where does Jake start emotionally at the beginning of the play, and where does he end? More importantly, what happens in the middle of the play that makes Jake's journey almost inevitable?

2. The character of Ana is practically the dramatic antithesis of Jake. How do their unparallel lives work together to justify the dramatic arc of the play?

3. When talking about the ten-minute play, Judith Royer said that it seemed to be most effective when the characters in the play were subtle and complex. How does the playwright achieve this in *Real Life?*

4. You might say the simple story line of the play is will Ana win the confidence of Jake in order to have a some sort of meaningful relationship? We know better than that. What details in the story begin nagging you that there is actually something much larger at stake?

Storm on Storm

By Gary Garrison

Characters:

> NORTON, M., 49. Has been struck by lightning twice.
>
> CHICKY, F., 48. Has quietly suffered through her husband being struck by lightning twice.

Time: Right now.

Setting: Norton and Chicky's backyard garden in Summit, New Jersey

> *Minutes after a summer deluge of rain.*
>
> *NORTON sits on a bench under a dome-shaped trellis covered with ivy that's interwoven with a wide variety of white and lavender ribbons, bows, and flowers: it's clearly over-decorated for a wedding. At his feet is a large bouquet of white, plastic roses tied at the stems with a lavender ribbon, resting upside down with the stems in the air.*
>
> *LIGHTS POP UP to reveal CHICKY, standing off to Norton's side, facing him, holding an open umbrella:*

CHICKY: (*fed up*) Alright, let's get it alllllllllll out, Norton, can we? All the feelings, all the thoughts, all the heartache and headache. Everything! Let's leave no stone unturned, leave nothing unsaid.

NORTON: Have you ever left anything unsaid? I don't think so, Chicky.

CHICKY: (*forging ahead*) Yes, I admit it. It's hard to live with a man that's been struck by lightning . . .(*hurriedly, before he says it*). . . TWICE. Yes, I'm frightened to be close to you when we're outside and there's a storm on the horizon – as there is now. And no, I don't understand – in fact NO ONE understands – why you seem to bring bad weather with you everywhere you go.

NORTON: Not everywhere. That's an exaggeration.

CHICKY: Everywhere, Norton! For three years thunder, lightning, rain, sleet and snow – not to mention the occasional hurricane-force winds – have followed you around like a puppy at your heels. You're banned from traveling in forty-three states. The Weather Channel has its own on-screen icon of you to let people know exactly where in the world you are so everyone else can make travel plans. And while the scholars, scientists, meteorologists, universities, newspapers and fifth grade science clubs all try to figure out why Norton Templer, Lawn Furniture Salesman from Summit, New Jersey is "weather provoking" – a term I still find uncomfortable, quite frankly – I spend my days trying to love you as if nothing has happened. But you, my sweet but troubled husband, refuse to let that happen.

NORTON: Because I'm miserable!

CHICKY: WE'RE ALL MISERABLE! The least of which is your young daughter that begged you for months to let her elope!

NORTON: I wanted my daughter to have a traditional wedding outside in our beautiful back yard. Why is that so hard for everyone to understand?

CHICKY: What you wanted was to prove to the world that your run of bad weather-luck was broken after visiting some feather-wearing, rattle-shaking, clay-pot-making Shaman from Sante Fe that sells gas on the weekends at an Exxon station to make ends meet.

NORTON: He had a gift!

CHICKY: He had an act! And it got you where, Norton? No where. So now that you've managed to rain out the rehearsal for your daughter's wedding, as well as seemingly flood three local counties due south of here, your daughter would like you to leave…and take the bad weather with you. If you want a wedding, she'll have a wedding. But she won't have a wedding that involves her father because that comes with a hundred per cent chance of rain, sleet, snow, hail or coastal swelling.

> *A huge sigh. Thunder rumbles in the distance, making them both very uneasy.*

NORTON: (*quietly*) I'm not going anywhere, Ms. Doom and Gloom. So go back in the house.

Norton miserably stares out at something in the distance, then maybe for the first time, notices the paper plate with a pile of chicken wings in his lap. Maybe for the first time, we notice the whole left side of him appears to be paralyzed. He grabs a chicken wing with his right hand and chews voraciously.

CHICKY: Wings, Norton?

NORTON: Don't start with me, Chicky.

CHICKY: Who's starting? I'm just looking at that pile of dissembled chicken in your lap and it gives one pause.

NORTON: "Gives one pause?" Who talks like that, Chicky? I don't talk like that. Do you talk like that? I don't recall you talking like that, but then again, the last three years have been a bit of a blur for me.

He bites into a wing voraciously and chews.

CHICKY: You've got a pile of fried chicken wings from the rehearsal dinner on your lap, Norton. You've been on a very strict diet for two years because of your health, and today, with a lap full of wings, it all goes to hell. How could I... ?

NORTON: It all went to hell wayyyyyyyyyyyyyyyyy before the wings. Three years ago I began my slow, torturous dissent into hell and today I finally sunk to the lowest of the low: the underbelly of Satan's ball-sack. That's how low, how deep in Hell I am.

CHICKY: Oh, for God's sake, "Satan's ball-sack," Norton? Where in the world did you get something like that?

NORTON: In the same store you bought "it gives one pause." You might know the store. It's right on the corner of "Who-Gives-A-Shit Street" and "Stop Bustin' My Balls Avenue."

CHICKY: You know, things would be just a little bit easier, if . . .

NORTON: What? If what? If three years ago I hadn't been struck by lightning but miraculously lived to tell the story? If I hadn't not a year later, almost to the date, been struck again by yet another bolt of lightning – something that's been documented only twice in all of history – but happens to me: Norton Templer, Lawn Furniture Salesman from Summit, New Jersey. Things would be so much easier if what, if that hadn't happened?

CHICKY: I was going to say things would be so much easier if you weren't so dramatic about everything.

NORTON: Oh, gosh. I'm sorry. Am I being dramatic? Hmmmm. Now why would that be? Could it be that my daughter decides at her wedding rehearsal that I should not walk her down the aisle to give her away, but in fact should stand approximately two hundred feet away from she and the groom – a fun fact she Googled last night when she couldn't sleep: what is the safe radius from a lightning strike? Two hundred feet. That would put me in the street, Chicky, to watch my daughter's wedding. And now I learn she'd like me to not be here at all! Or is it that my wife, who's concerned about me eating chicken wings, being dramatic and saying things like "Satan's ball-sack," won't risk sitting with me in the open air. She won't lower her umbrella, which is probably more of a lightning rod than the one she's married to, to sit with her husband and talk about his problems.

> *In a burst of courage and anger, Chicky drops her opened umbrella to the ground and marches to the bench.*

CHICKY: Fine! You want talk, talk. Leave no stone unturned: here we go.

> *She plops herself next to Norton and stares out. Silence, then:*

CHICKY (*cont.*): You're not talking.

> *A huge sigh, this time from Norton. He leans his head gently on her shoulders.*

NORTON: What am I going to do?

> *Another rumble of thunder. Norton reaches into his jacket, pulls out an envelope, pulls out the letter, hands it to Chicky. She reads, then crumples it in her hands.*

CHICKY: So they don't want you at your high school reunion? Who cares? They should be so lucky to have a storm or two around that deadly dull event. Besides, were you really looking forward to seeing Mimi Delfont in those tight, black stirrup stretch pants providing our annual viewing of suburban camel toe? I think not, Norton. That was never my idea of a good time.

NORTON: Danny Tomlin always enjoyed that view.

CHICKY: Danny Tomlin's wanted to have a vagina since he was in the ninth grade. Of course he enjoyed the view.

> *Norton smiles for the very first time, then pecks her cheek with a kiss. He takes another letter out and hands it to her. She reads quickly.*

CHICKY (*cont.*): So you'll get another job.

NORTON: Can't blame them, really. Can't really sell lawn furniture if it pours rain on you and your clients every time you step outside. Sales were beginning to drop off. My novelty was wearing off too. I mean, how far can you really go with The Human Lightning Rod. You can't blame them.

CHICKY: They got a lot of good press out of you.

NORTON: Yeah, and I got some place to go every day. So I think we're even. Now what? I don't know. I don't know anything – maybe for the first time in my life.

CHICKY: Maybe that's not so bad, Norton.

> *He takes another letter out.*

CHICKY (*cont.*): How many more of these do you have?

NORTON: Last one. Swear.

> *He hands it to her. She reads it.*

CHICKY: Would you want to really live in Oregon?

NORTON: Well, they need the rain. And apparently, a lot of it. Of course, I can't guarantee them anything, but my odds are good, to say the least. And they're offering good money.

CHICKY: Oregon? I don't know, Norton. I've never even heard of someone being from Oregon. Have you? I mean, I know it's a state, but have you actually ever heard someone say, "I'm from Oregon." In all my years, I don't think I have.

NORTON: Yeah, it's probably not such a good idea. (*crumpling the paper*) I'm glad you're on my side, kid.

CHICKY: (*quietly*) Me too…It's a little lonely sometimes, but I'm where I belong.

NORTON: (*defensive*) Well, I tell you to go out, go to movie, see friends, but you never do. I can manage. I've still got one side of me that works. Served a whole plate of chicken wings for myself. See? You should go out. You should see friends.

CHICKY: Friends I see, Norton. I'm lonely being right beside you because you're often not there. Even when you're here, you're not here. When you were struck by lightning, I saw you leave the earth, lift right up and float way far away.

> She stands, almost courageously takes a few steps out into the wide open.

CHICKY (*cont.*): And every day since then, I look into those big, bulbous clouds, half expecting to see you float back down. But of course that never happens, and I'm sad about it, Norton. Sad that ever since you became "weather provoking," things have been bad in a way I never expected: a real storm on storm.

NORTON: What's that mean?

CHICKY: There's the weather on the outside and maybe it's because of you, maybe it's not. Who knows? Maybe it's all just a coincidence. But then we have the weather on the inside of the house: and that's absolutely because of you. There's a storm building up in our home – a violent, horrible storm that's gonna explode on us. It's gonna rain down misery and sadness all over us. Because whether you see it or not, whether you feel or not, I still love you. But Norton, I need you to love me, or so help me God, I'll leave you.

NORTON: But I still love you. Of course I still love you.

CHICKY: Then why do you bring the cold in? It's freezing in our house; this beautiful home we built together. There's no warmth in there, anywhere. Not in any corner of any room. You're making it unlivable in there.

NORTON: I know I'm cold. I'm cold because I'm broken. I am half a man. Half of me doesn't work, Chicky. That's what lightning does to you, IF you survive. And the part of me that really needs to work, has no life at all. Try living with that.

CHICKY: Frankly, I'm a little glad it's gone.

NORTON: What?!

CHICKY: Well, because it's always about the putz, isn't it? Everything's about the putz. Is it going to work, is it not going to work? How long is it going to work before it begins to feel like work? All in all, I think it's over-rated.

NORTON: That's easy for you to say.

CHICKY: Norton, what are you talking about? So you don't have a penis; I have no breasts because of my cancer. We're a perfect match. We always were, even before. There was a time when we didn't know each other that way – the physical way. And you loved me and I loved you with every hope and desire we had for each other. Go back to those days. Love me with your eyes, Norton. Love me with your sweet smile. Love me with everything you have, whatever that is. I can live a life-time with a simple touch of your hand and the look of desire in your eye; but I can't live a moment more without it.

> *With his right hand, Norton touches his wife's cheek sweetly,*
> *then kisses her and looks deep in her eyes. Finally:*

NORTON: If lightning strikes again, I gotta have one last look in these eyes before I go…

CHICKY: No one could be that unlucky. Lightning won't strike again – at least, not that way.

NORTON: If that minister is still around, get him out here. I want to marry you all over again.

*Chicky smiles brightly, then walks briskly back towards the
house. She turns back:*

CHICKY: Norton, what should I tell your daughter?

A long moment, then:

NORTON: Tell her she's invited to our wedding.

Lights fade slowly on their smiles.

Blackout.

End of play.

Reader's Questions

1. What do you find comic in the play? What's absurd in the play?
   How does it work in balance to the drama? And what does it do to
   the overall momentum and arc of the play?

2. This is a traditional three-part structured play with exposition,
   rising action layered with complications, crisis and climax. Can you
   identify those parts of the play? How does one lead to the other?

3. This is a play about a relationship. What indicates the relationship's
   history? Is it a good relationship? Bad relationship? Troubled? Two
   people in relationship often develop their own particular language
   of speaking to one another. How do you understand Chicky and
   Norton's relationship through the way they speak to one another?

4. There is a third character in the play that has its own personality.
   What's that character? How does it complicate the story? Can the
   story only be told if it's present, or could the story be told without
   it?

Off Hand

By Michel Wallerstein

Characters:

> WOMAN, (early 60's). Tall, with a commanding presence. Still attractive. Dressed simply, yet elegantly. Wears just the right amount of expensive looking jewelry. There's a nervous energy about her, and comments about art are quick and matter of fact. This is the first time she's out alone in public since her husband's death.

> MAN, (late 20's). Medium build. Good looking. Charming. Passionate when talks. Gets easily carried away. He appears to be self-confident but is vulnerable. Dressed in dark jeans and a dress shirt, trying to "fit in" the art world.

Time: Today.

Setting: An art gallery in New York City.

> *Lights up on Woman looking disapprovingly at a painting stage right (the paintings of the gallery are the audience). She is carrying a catalogue, opens it and stares back at the painting.*

> *Man sits on a gallery bench and observes Woman. She doesn't notice him. She is still at the painting in front of her. She frowns.*

WOMAN: (*Disapprovingly.*) Please.

> *She shrugs and moves on. She now stops (center stage) admiringly in front of the next painting. She clearly likes that painting.*

WOMAN: Ahhh! Yes. (Steps back for a better view.)

MAN: So you like that one?

WOMAN: (*Annoyed, her back to him.*) Yes.

MAN: It's beautiful.

WOMAN: (*Still not facing him.*) Yes.

MAN: And you like it better than this one?

WOMAN: Without question.

MAN: (*Studying the one she likes.*) Hmmmm. What do you like so much about it?

WOMAN: I don't know. I guess how the artist brings her soul to...

MAN: ...her?

WOMAN: (*Matter of fact.*) Yes. The artist is a woman.

MAN: Really? How do you know that? (*Reads the signature on the painting.*) R. Bastian. R could be for Robert or Ronald or a ton of other names.

WOMAN: I recognize a woman's depth and sensitivity. (*Pointing to the previous painting.*) This one, on the other hand, was definitely painted by a man. A man with a dark and twisted vision of the world.

MAN (*Looking closely at the painting, defensively.*) At least he signed his full name. Andrew Barton. No ambiguity there.

WOMAN: (*Looking at the painting with him.*) No soul either. No surprise. Nothing. (*At the one she likes.*) Whereas this painting is filled with substance and meaning ... It's far too spiritual and inspired to be the work of a man.

MAN: Oh, so Michelangelo or ...Caravaggio or El Greco: they weren't spiritual or inspired because they were men?

WOMAN: Those great artists lived in different times. A man could not paint like that today. Not in a society only interested in the Dow Jones, MTV and dot coms...Now, if you'll excuse me.

> *Woman moves the to the next painting. Man follows her. She wishes he'd leave her alone.*

MAN (*Gentler.*) I'm sorry. I didn't mean to be so blunt.

WOMAN: (*Gentler.*) We're all entitled to our opinions.

MAN: That's right…So…How can you be so sure R. Bastian is a woman? There are no pictures in the bio. And no pronouns are ever used to describe her.

Woman now notices Man is attractive.

WOMAN: (*Girlish.*) Well, I don't like to brag…(*In a loud whisper.*)….but I know her personally.

MAN: Nothing wrong with a little bragging…So what does the R stand for?

WOMAN: (*With a perfect French pronunciation*). Renee. Renee Bastien.

MAN: (*Trying to sound as "French" as her.*) Renee Bastien…Hmmm? So what do you think Renee's trying to tell us with her painting?

Woman walks back to the previous painting.

WOMAN: Well, I…I'm not sure she's trying to tell us anything. The image is…magical, almost surreal, like the early works of Dali. The liberating hand…

MAN: (*Looking at the painting.*) That hand, yes. It's nice.

WOMAN: Nice? It's phenomenal. That hand is power. It's about to liberate the body from its imprisonment, to let it breathe finally, by throwing open the window. The window to freedom, to a new life!

MAN: (*Takes a closer look at the painting.*) Hmmm. Looks to me as if the hand is closing the window, not opening it.

WOMAN: Rubbish! Look at that light. The sun is shining outside the window. There's a gentle, westerly breeze. See how those branches swing to the left? And on the oak tree, a little bluebird is sticking out like in a Rousseau painting.

MAN: (*Trying to see.*) Oh, yeah. I see it.

WOMAN: And it's chirping.

MAN: You can't really tell it's chirping. It's too small.

WOMAN: (*Definite.*) It's chirping, alright? I know it is. And it's perfectly clear: the woman in the painting is opening the window. To get air. To begin again. There maybe a slight hesitation in the movement, I'll grant you that, but the decision to open that window has been made years ago and now finally, she knows that nothing can stop her anymore. Not even her own fear.

MAN: Oh. So this is a woman's hand?

WOMAN: Of course it is.

MAN: (*Biting.*) Don't you think it's kind of square and rugged? And those veins.

WOMAN: Veins?!

MAN: You don't see veins like that on a woman's hand.

WOMAN: There are no veins on this hand.

MAN (looking closer.) And look, you can even see a few hairs.

WOMAN: Hair! Where?

MAN: (*Pointing.*) There.

WOMAN: That's no hair. That's just…a careless brush stroke.

MAN: More like six or seven! No. I'm sorry. That is a man's hand.

WOMAN: This is my hand, alright? ! I posed for it. She painted *my* hand. (*Places her hand close up to the painting.*) And there is no hair on *my* hand.

MAN: Lady, that couldn't possibly be your hand.

WOMAN: And why on earth not?

MAN: (*Angry.*) Look at it! Yours is much prettier than that. So fragile and elegant. That is a hard working, tough man's hand. But if it's really yours, the artist should be shot. (*She turns her back on him.*) I'm sorry. I got carried away. A bad habit of mine…Let me make it up to you… smooth things over with a coffee across the street.

WOMAN: Thank you. I don't think so. I'd just like to enjoy this exhibition. Alone. If you don't mind.

MAN: Of course. I understand. I'm sorry.

> *Woman walks to the next painting. Man stares at her. She senses it.*

WOMAN (*Facing him.*) You're staring.

MAN: Sorry.

WOMAN: It's rude.

MAN: I just find you…interesting.

WOMAN: Young man, are you flirting with me?

MAN: Well, you are a very attractive woman.

WOMAN: And almost twice your age. (*Looks at one of the rings on her fingers.*) If you think I'm one of those rich ladies who spend their time lunching and attending every gallery opening in town, you're quite mistaken. I'm not rich. These rings are fake. All of them. Not worth a dime.

MAN: For heaven's sake, so now I'm after you for your money?

WOMAN: I'm sorry. I….it's just that men your age should be interested in younger women.

MAN: (*Ironic.*) Sure. The young should stick together.

> *Woman shyly walks away. He stares at her again.*

WOMAN: You're staring again. Why?

MAN: Habit. I spend a lot of time in places like these and study whoever walks in. I make up stories about them. About their lives. About what brought them here today.

WOMAN: What do you think brought me here today?

MAN: Well, in your case, I already know: you came to see your hand.

WOMAN (*Humbled.*) Perhaps it isn't my hand.

MAN: So you didn't pose for it?

WOMAN: I did. Sort of. A friend of mine took pictures of my hand one day. (*Hold it out.*) He shot two entire rolls. Just of my hand. Imagine that...he said that a painter he knew was looking for the hand of perfect elegance and refinement. I was flattered. At my age, I couldn't believe that anything about my appearance could be "perfect." I was thrilled my friend thought of me, of my hand...(*Looks at the painting.*) Apparently Renee Bastien didn't agree with him. (*Faces Man, after a beat.*) But I needed to believe that was me up there, or at least a part of me. I've had a hard week. Month. Let's just say I've had a hard year and I wanted to feel special today.

MAN: And I blew all that for you, didn't I? What a jerk.

WOMAN: Don't worry about it.

MAN: There's nothing worse than robbing someone of their dream.

WOMAN: (*Walking away, decidedly.*) It was a small dream. A stupid one.

MAN: I lied to you.

WOMAN: My dear, young man, you haven't known me long enough to lie to me.

MAN: I wasn't really trying to figure you out. When I saw you looking at that painting, with your heart and not your mind, I knew I wanted your response.

WOMAN: Response?

MAN: I'm Andrew Barton. The painter with the "dark and twisted vision of the world."

WOMAN: Oh, my.

MAN: I painted the painting you hate.

WOMAN: I...I don't really hate it, just...

MAN: Yes, you do. Everybody does. This is my first exhibition. And I've been watching people ignore my work all week and go straight to R. Bastian's stupid hand. Sorry. And since the exhibit ends tonight, I just wanted to know what was wrong with my work? How come no one ever stops in front of my painting and goes: "Ah, yes."

WOMAN: So I robbed you of *your* dream?

MAN: Yeah, but I'm used to it.

WOMAN: No one ever gets used to that. No one ever should.

MAN: My art teachers told me I was wasting my time, that I should quit art school and get a job.

WOMAN: I'm sure someone must like your work or they wouldn't be showing it here. Someone obviously believes in you.

MAN: The owner of the gallery is my aunt. (*She chuckles.*) My parents cut me off once they found out I was studying more art than law. So she felt sorry for me. I sold my car, my stereo, my t.v. and everything I own just to be able to paint and have this exhibition. Not a good move, I'd say. Wouldn't you?

WOMAN: I don't know what to say.

MAN: My mother didn't even show up.

WOMAN: (*Gentle.*) I'm sure she's sorry.

MAN: You would have shown up, if...

> *He stops, feeling he's gone too far. They look at each other for a short, awkward moment.*

WOMAN: (*Light.*) You're a nice, young man. And I do see talent in your painting...

MAN: ...despite my dark and twisted vision of the world, huh?

WOMAN: (*Looks at painting*). A great, big foot crushing Planet Earth. Yes. I'd say it's dark.

MAN: It was meant to be ironic.

WOMAN: You don't say.

An awkward silence.

MAN: Sorry you've had such a bad year.

WOMAN: Well, it's over now. My husband...he was very sick...I nursed him day in, day out. I wanted to, of course, but it was very...He...he finally died last month. Everyone says it's much better this way – no more pain. Maybe for them. My whole world's collapsed, as if that foot of yours smashed it to pieces.

MAN: I'm sorry.

WOMAN: (*Studying his painting.*) Is there...Yes! Is there a hand holding that foot?

MAN: (*Excited.*) I knew it! I knew you'd finally see it! The hand is superimposed on top of the foot, lifting it away.

WOMAN: And ...isn't there someone...trying to escape from that crushing foot?

MAN: Yes! That's right.

WOMAN: I think it's a woman...

MAN: (*Interjecting. Grinning.*) ... or a man.

WOMAN: She's trying to pull herself out between the forth and fifth toe. Of course, I wouldn't see all this if I weren't looking from exactly this angle.

MAN: Exactly!

WOMAN: Very Magritte. (*Looking now, more intensely.*) And that hand...that hand is liberating the planet, isn't it?

MAN: You got it!

WOMAN: (*Softly.*) So the woman is struggling for nothing.

MAN: Or the man. Could be. It could be all in his or her mind. But the liberating hand is definitely a woman's hand. (*Takes her hand gently.*) Not unlike yours. As a matter of fact, it's just like yours.

WOMAN: (*Wanting to believe*). Do you think?

MAN: I'm positive. Look at it: the same fine, elongated fingers. The same elegance. (*Pointing triumphantly at this painting.*) This is your hand.

WOMAN: Extraordinary. Yes. Yes…I think I see it. I do.

> *Woman and Man stand close and look at the painting together.*
>
> *Lights fade.*
>
> *End.*

Reader's Questions

1. We've talked about creating interesting behavior for the characters that we write as means of expressing their emotional life. What behavior defines these characters? And how does their behavior propel the story forward?

2. One of the structural suggestions I made when writing your ten-minute play was to begin in the middle of the story – forgetting about what we'd all think is a "beginning" and jump instead right into the action. How does the playwright do this in *Off Hand?* What's the beginning beat or scene that's missing? How and where do we hear of it later in the play?

3. As people, our choice of words and language often reflects back on our character, histories, education, religion, cultural influences and age. What do we know, or, can we assume about Man and Woman based solely on their use of language?

4. The hand in the painting is a plot point in the story, but also a metaphor for what's not discussed overtly in the play. What does the hand represent between these two people and how is the idea of that woven throughout the story?

Crimes Against Humanity

By Ross Maxwell

Characters:

>   Flora, 24

>   Michael, 19

Time: Late in the afternoon

Setting: A small messy office

>   *LIGHTS UP ON:*

>   *A small messy office. FLORA (24) has been going through drawers, packing a duffel bag. There are stacks of paperwork on a desk. She's dressed very young cosmopolitan business woman.*

>   *MICHAEL (19), her brother, stands in the doorway with a backpack slung over his shoulder. He's dressed much more "street," and looks out of place in her office space.*

FLORA: You really shouldn't be here.

MICHAEL: You're right, it <u>was</u> really nice of me to come all the way into the city to bring you back your stuff. You're welcome.

FLORA: You have five minutes, Michael, and then you gotta go. I'm serious. This is me talking seriously.

MICHAEL: This is you talking seriously.

FLORA: Five minutes.

MICHAEL: Five minutes.

FLORA: –and I didn't <u>ask</u> you to come all the way into the city.

MICHAEL: No, Mom had the wood spoon out, pointing it in my face and <u>telling</u> me I <u>had</u> to come into the city and give you your shit back because she raised such a fuckin gentleman. Whaddaya-gonna-do?

He holds out the backpack. She looks at it, sighs, and grabs it.

MICHAEL: You don't think I got better ways to spend my time?

FLORA: You really want me to answer that?

Flora looks in the backpack.

FLORA: Oh Jesus, I left this stuff at Mom's on purpose.

MICHAEL: Why would you leave a bag full of your old diaries at Mom's?

FLORA: You read them on the subway ride here, didn't you.

MICHAEL: (*indignant*) No I didn't read your stupid diaries on the way here. (*beat*) I read that shit years ago.

FLORA: I need you to take them back to Mom's for me.

MICHAEL: What? Hell no I'm not just taking em back there after coming all the way in from Brooklyn. At night. In the heat. Plus, Mom'll still be standing on the stoop with that big ass wood spoon of hers. I'm not giving her any excuses.

FLORA: Fine. Look, whatever. Just leave it here then, I guess. They'll make something of it.

MICHAEL: Who'll make something outta what?

She turns and stands in front of the desk with her duffel back on it.

FLORA: Well, look, thanks for– (*beat*) –you know– (*beat*) Anyway.

MICHAEL: Anyway.

Beat. She looks at him. He leans a little to look past her at what she's doing.

FLORA: You can probably go now, Michael.

MICHAEL: So this is the UN, huh? Looks bigger on TV.

FLORA: This is not the UN.

MICHAEL: But I thought you were such the big deal UN intern–

FLORA: (*overlapping*) – I never said I was a *big deal*– This is <u>an</u> office of the Human Rights Council of the United Nations. Happy? All clear now?

MICHAEL: You work this late cuz they give you a lot of work?

FLORA: No. I work late because I have initiative.

MICHAEL: What's that mean?

FLORA: It means I don't spend my time chillin with my boys on Flatbush looking for kids to sell cheap weed to.

MICHAEL: (*loudly, as if to a hidden mic*) I don't know what you're talking about, Flora. I don't use or associate myself with illegal drugs and/or drug related substances of any kind.

FLORA: The room's not bugged, you idiot.

MICHAEL: Oh, so you're just being nasty for my benefit. You know something, you're starting to sound just like they <u>say</u> you sound.

FLORA: Who's "they"?

MICHAEL: Girls back in the neighborhood sayin you don't call none of them anymore. How you think you're so big and special now.

FLORA: You know what you can tell when they say that? I <u>am</u> big and special now. I'm up here working on big and special things. I'm not back in Brooklyn, sitting on the stoop, braiding my hair, dressing like a 12-year-old hooker, waiting for someone to knock me up.

MICHAEL: I <u>will</u> tell them that.

FLORA: You go ahead.

MICHAEL: Only, you know–I'll make it sound nicer cuz some of those girls are fine.

FLORA: Look, we already hung out at Mom's tonight… so, I mean, thanks and all, but I need you to leave now.

MICHAEL: So what big and special stuff you working on that you're in such a hurry?

FLORA: Michael–

MICHAEL: What, is it top secret or something?

FLORA: Do you actually want to know, or is this just some set-up to knock me down?

MICHAEL: I asked, didn't I? Damn, why you being so nasty to me?

FLORA: I work with a human rights commission to help stop forced disappearances.

MICHAEL: Hmm. Well, that sounds– pretty boring–

FLORA: (*simultaneously*) –"boring," yeah, I figured. These are crimes against humanity. South American mostly. People being abducted, erased.

MICHAEL: Hell, forget South America. You got people getting disappeared out in Brooklyn. You remember my buddy Tink?

> *Michael starts flipping through some of the things on her desk. As she's talking, he gets to the duffel bag.*

FLORA: Yeah, except <u>I'm</u> talking about people that aren't asking for it. Activists, artists, women. Whole families. But since nobody cares, it's hard to get any press attention here.

MICHAEL: What's in this bag?

FLORA: Nothing's in that bag–

MICHAEL: What, is this, like, your gym bag or something? You working out now–?

FLORA: Michael, stop messing things up–

MICHAEL: This looks like that time you tried to run away from home and you got as far as Atlantic and–

FLORA: Stop going through my stuff. I'm being serious–

MICHAEL: Hey, what's this–

> *He pulls out a passport.*

MICHAEL: When'd you get a passport?

Pause. She looks at him.

MICHAEL: What are you doing, Flora?

FLORA: What do mean, what am I doing? I'm not <u>doing</u> anything. I'm standing here wondering why my little brother thinks he has the right to interrogate me.

MICHAEL: You're here in the city late, packing a bag. You want me to take these old *diaries* of yours <u>back</u> to Mom's where you <u>purposely</u> left them... you going away someplace I don't know about?

Pause.

FLORA: You wouldn't understand–

MICHAEL: Cuz I'm just so stupid and you're so big and special.

FLORA: I'm making a political statement, Michael, and I know that's not your thing.

MICHAEL: What?

FLORA: Politics. Having a bigger picture. Understanding or caring about what's going on outside your five block radius.

MICHAEL: It must be pretty hard for you to have such a trashy, narrow-minded loser brother.

FLORA: (*pointedly*) Sometimes. Yeah.

MICHAEL: How's running away from home a political statement?

FLORA: I'm not running away. I'm disappearing.

MICHAEL: I'm not so stupid you can't just explain it.

She starts to re-pack the clothes into the duffel bag. She considers how to start:

FLORA: I'm kidnapping myself. These days, media coverage is all that matters. We've been in the news dealing with corruption in the governments down there, how little they try, how they don't care. So

I'm going to disappear under mysterious circumstances and that's going to bring media attention to the issue. I'm leaving some "clues" behind to incriminate the right people, then I walk out the front door, making sure to say good-night to the security guard on-camera. I walk a couple blocks down, turn a corner, and disappear. I'm supposed to meet my friend Nina at a bar in an hour so when I don't show up, she'll get worried, and… it'll go from there.

Pause.

MICHAEL: <u>That's</u> your big and special work? Are you fuckin nuts?

FLORA: I knew you wouldn't get it–

MICHAEL: Of course I *get* it, it's just stupid. And sick. And, what– you just never show up again?

She shakes her head.

MICHAEL: What about your friends and your family? What about them?

FLORA: (*bittersweet*) Oh, Michael… (*beat*) What <u>about</u> them?

MICHAEL: You mean if I didn't come here, tonight at Mom's would've been the last time?

FLORA: I thought dinner with Mom was a good last time to have– until she got drunk and started yelling–

MICHAEL: She wasn't drunk. *Jesus*, you're such a snob–

FLORA: Only now because of you, we have a problem. You're on-camera coming into the building, so if you don't want to be a part of this, then you need to go now and be on-camera leaving before me.

MICHAEL: I'll tell on you to Mom.

FLORA: No, you won't.

MICHAEL: Why not?

FLORA: Because you love me, and because if you ruin this for me, you'll never see me again. I'll find other ways to vanish. I won't ever come back to the neighborhood again.

MICHAEL: *You don't come back now!* You really do think you're a whole lot better than us, don't you.

FLORA: In some ways. No. I don't think that, but I don't belong there. Maybe you do, maybe you like that, but I have to make a bigger world for myself and this is how I'm going to do it.

MICHAEL: And this is really gonna help your UN cause? Just cuz some pretty intern went missing?

FLORA: Did you just call me pretty?

MICHAEL: –cuz some dog-faced intern went missing? I'm serious, Flora. I'm talking serious here. Don't do this. Why you always gotta make some big noise of things? Fine. You're a big city deal and I don't know outside my five blocks, but you know what? I know enough not to fuck over the people I love.

> *Pause. She looks at him.*

MICHAEL: (*crushed*) Oh. (*beat*) I was assuming too much there, huh. I got it. I gotcha.

FLORA: I didn't say that. Don't hear that from what I'm saying, but, I gotta make a clean break of this–

MICHAEL: "A clean break?" Oh my God, I get it. You think you can get high and mighty with all the politics and I'm too dumb to see what you're really all about? You're not disappearing because of South America. You're disappearing because of you.

FLORA: I'm disappearing because of you. And Mom. And my whole, everything. I finally figured it out. I gotta amputate everything off completely and start over someplace totally new. It's just what I have to do to survive, you know what I mean?

MICHAEL: <u>No</u>. (beat) I don't get how you survive without the neighborhood and the people you grew up with. See, that's what I figured out. Why am I out with my boys up and down Flatbush? Cuz I <u>like</u> Flatbush! Fuck the world beyond it! It <u>is</u> the world!

FLORA: It's not mine.

> *She picks up the duffel bag.*

FLORA: I gotta go, Michael. Five minutes, remember? Which means you have to go first.

MICHAEL: That's it, huh. I can't talk you out of it?

FLORA: I'm already gone.

> *He picks up the back-pack with the diaries and puts it over his shoulder.*

MICHAEL: On second thought, you know, I think I am gonna haul this shit back out to Brooklyn. You know, for Mom.

FLORA: Yeah.

MICHAEL: Well, I guess, good luck then… liberating South America, or, you know, freeing the people from deception or whatever cloak-and-dagger bullshit you're clinging onto.

FLORA: That's very inspiring, thank you.

MICHAEL: Well, you know some of us aren't gifted with language. Some of us got other qualities that make us worthwhile.

> *As she speaks, Flora picks up a few last things. The busy work takes her eyes away from Michael in the background.*

FLORA: I really wish I could explain this to you, but I don't think you can understand it. And I don't mean that like you're not smart enough to understand it. You're a smart guy, Michael. You and Mom are going to be fine. What I mean is, if you could only see what this is going to be like from my perspective, you'd see it's not such a bad thing after all–

> *She looks up. Michael's gone. Pause.*

FLORA: Maybe you'd see it like I do. (*beat*) It's a human rights issue.

> *She stands with the duffel bag on her shoulder. She looks at her watch. Beat. She looks at the door. Beat. She looks at her watch. Beat.*

> *LIGHTS OUT.*

The Fisherman

By Jayme McGhan

Characters:

      Carl Swanson- 56.

      Jenny Swanson- 30. Carl's Niece. Police Officer.

Time: Present. Late Fall. Dusk.

Setting: Bloomington, Minnesota. The shoreline of the Minnesota River.

> *Lights up on the shoreline of the Minnesota River. It is evening, dusk, late fall. A forgotten and decaying dock hangs over the muddy shore and out in to the water. Carl, a man in his fifties, sits alone on the dock. There are a number of empty beer bottles around his feet along with a few dead carp. He is dressed warmly and has a blanket over his lap. He holds a fishing pole. He looks up, then dumps some of his beer in to the water.*

CARL: A gift for my friends the fish. The good fish. Thank you. From the bottom of my…I want to say…I want to express my gratitude. (*he drinks*) Twenty-seven pound carp on eight-pound test. Remember that Charlie? Fish was so big…had it's own area code. Twenty-minutes it took. No net or nothing. Just plopped it right up on the dock and cut that fish's stomach from gills to asshole. Spilled it all. Blood all over the… running back in to the river. You remember that? Spilled all that blood. Wasn't that hard, was it? (*pause*) Can't catch nothing down here no more! Goddamn fish are…you got no courage no more! You're all afraid of the goddamn stupid carp!

> *JENNY enters from a path in the tree line. She wears a police uniform.*

JENNY: Carl? Uncle Carl? Jesus. You must have cleaned out Al's entire stock of High Life.

CARL: Sun's going down. Fish aint biting no more. (*pause*) How'd you find me?

JENNY: You and dad've been fishing this same spot for forty years. (*she looks around*) I haven't been down here since I was a girl. Looks pretty much the same. Docks nearly rotten through.

CARL: Still keeps me dry. That's about all you can ask of it.

JENNY: How long you been out here?

CARL: Getting colder out.

JENNY: Colder than a polar bear's nuts.

CARL: Winter's near. It'll all be frozen soon enough. Never could bring myself to it. Cutting a hole in the river, sitting in twenty-below weather for a few measly sunfish. Charlie could do it. Charlie loves ice fishing. Not me though. Skins not thick enough. Either that, or I'm just not as thick-headed as your dad. They stop looking for me yet?

JENNY: Are you kidding? The whole state is looking for you. The whole country.

CARL: Huh. You coming to take me in?

    Silence.

JENNY: Catch anything?

CARL: Few carp. Shit fish. The good ones don't bite here no more 'cause of them. Scare's all the good ones away. Sons of bitch bullies think they can get away with anything they want.

JENNY: Using crawlers?

CARL: Ran out of 'em a while ago. Just an old daredevil now. (*pause*) Dispatch know you're down here?

JENNY: Nah. I'm off duty. Should I radio it in and tell them? You plan on running?

CARL: Nah. Bad knees.

JENNY: You look like hell, Carl.

CARL: I feel alright.

CARL downs the rest of his beer and throws it in the river.

JENNY: Pollute the Minnesota River with Wisconsin beer? That's sacrilegious. What would Dad say if he saw you do that?

> *CARL cracks open another beer, hands one to JENNY who sits and drinks.*

CARL: Don't matter. (*pause*) How's Linda and the boys?

JENNY: She's…she's scared, you know? They got a media camp set up in front of the house. Not to mention the police. The F.B.I. The F.A.A. She couldn't handle all the–she went to stay with your son in Eau Claire. You should call her, Carl.

CARL: She knows I love her. She knows.

JENNY: Listen, I've been talking to some lawyers.

CARL: Lawyers, huh? Hell of a lot of good that would do me.

JENNY: It's bad, Carl. Really bad. They're calling it the worst crime in Minnesota history.

CARL: No. Not the worst. (*pause*) Don't suppose you could run up to Al's and get me some more crawlers?

JENNY: You know I can't do that.

CARL: Didn't think so. (*pause*) How's Matthew? The kids?

JENNY: Gotta' love 'em. Matthew's still at the power plant. Brandon turned five yesterday. Can't stop fighting with his older sister.

CARL: Sounds like a Swanson boy to me.

JENNY: Little bastards is what they are. I get home from my shift, hauling in drunks all day, breaking up domestics…not three feet in the door and they're screaming like a couple of raped apes. I prefer the criminals.

CARL: Apple don't fall too far from the tree. You used to shit a brick if Charlie didn't get you a treat in the bait shop…hollering in the back of his pickup like the world was coming to an end all the way to the river.

(*CARL reels in, then casts*) Remember that old nook under the overpass? You kids caught some beautiful largemouths down there.

JENNY: Yeah, they were something.

CARL: You remember what I taught you?

JENNY: Eagle claw with a Maloney stink bait. Cast past the birch grove. Pull every few feet. Hook 'em hard. Don't let them get…

CARL: …too far in to the current. Good girl. (*pause*)

JENNY: God damnit. God damn you, Carl.

CARL: Thirty-five years. Thirty-five years we put in to that airline Jenny. That's all we know, your dad and me. Fixing airplane doors and fishing the Minnesota. (*pause*) Two more years and I'd have nothing to do but toss lines into the water. Nothing to do but drink a few Millers and reel in the whoppers. Don't need no fanciness, just some water and a hook. But I can't do that without a pension, can I? Can't even keep my home or my boat or my…(*pause*) Fire five-hundred of my friends, two years from their retirement? Steal their pension? Steal their lives? Give their work to some snot-nosed shits for a quarter of the pay? All so some fat fucking pigs can get some more slop in their trough? (*CARL spits in to the river*) That right there is your worst crime in Minnesota history.

JENNY: You killed seventeen people.

CARL: Seventeen shit fish.

JENNY: Seventeen people Carl! I don't care who they are! CEO's, Executives, Directors–you put explosives on their airplane and pushed the goddamn button!

CARL: They blew up my life! They blew up Charlie's life. Jimmy's, and Harriet's, and Tom's–all of us–my friends. Five-hundred people Jenny. The year before that, nine-hundred ticket agents. The year before that, fourteen-hundred baggage handlers. (*pause*) You can only kick a bear in the ass for so long before he turns around and mauls you.

CARL reels in and casts.

JENNY: They're all calling you a terrorist. The local television, the national media and newspapers…they all want your head on a stake.

CARL: And what about you Jenny? You think that's what I am?

JENNY: I think…I think there's a lot of folks who do think that.

CARL: I don't care what they think. You're my kin.

JENNY: I don't know what to think. I don't know anything. (*pause*) You know, funny thing is, there's a lot of folks who…who think the world of you. There's a lot of folks…cops even…most of my friends…a lot folks who think you should be given a parade. It's sick, isn't it? (*pause*) You got the corporate world scrambling. They're shitting their pants. Government too. All the way up to the fed. They're all scared they're going to be next. (*pause*) Ah hell Carl. I'm an officer of the law. I'm not allowed to think like that. The only thing I do is take people who break the law and bring them to jail. The rest is past me. I'm not a judge and jury. I aint God.

CARL: Neither were they.

JENNY: You got to tell me the truth. I don't want any bullshit answers so don't lie. I'll know if you're lying. (*pause*) Dad…he hasn't been, the last few days…right, you know? Not sad, not down like you'd think. Happy. He's actually smiling. I haven't seen him smile in…God knows? (*she takes CARL by the hand*) Did he know? Did my dad know?

Silence.

CARL: You don't want to know that Jenny.

JENNY: Tell me.

CARL: No. Charlie didn't do anything.

JENNY: Thank God.

CARL: But he didn't say anything either. (*pause*)

JENNY: He knew? He knew you were going to do it?

CARL: Most of them did.

JENNY: Oh God. Oh my God.

CARL: Charlie's been put in the same barrel as the rest of us. He's got the same blood in his eyes. (*CARL reels in, casts again*) I pushed the button. Yeah, I did it. But I'll tell you something, there were five-hundred people holding the detonator. Hell, most of the country was holding it with us. (*JENNY fondles her handcuffs*) You should be proud of your pop. He did a good thing.

JENNY: (*removing her handcuffs*) No, Carl...he didn't. You have the right...you have the right to–

CARL: Remain silent? Just like your dad. Just like Tom and Scott, Gary, Julie, Mark...all of them. They all stayed silent, and they all will. What are you going to do, arrest every one of them?

JENNY: Anything you say can...can and will be–

CARL: You know I won't go with you.

JENNY: That doesn't much matter. I'm taking you.

CARL: Taking me where? To justice? There's no such thing! It doesn't exist! It took me fifty-six years to figure that out! Not your law, not your government, none of them! Number one rule in nature, protect what's yours...eat the other fish before he eats you!

> *JENNY takes CARL's hand and puts it behind his back. She locks a cuff on to his wrist.*

JENNY: You have the right to an–

CARL: You can't have me, honey. I don't belong there and I'm not going. (*she puts his other hand behind his back. He pulls away*) Let me fish a little while longer. (*she tries to use force, twisting his arm behind his back. He grabs her wrist and puts her in a choke-hold*) Stop it goddamnit! Stop it!

JENNY: You're assaulting an officer, that's a federal offense!

CARL: Do you really think that matters? Now, leave me be.

> *JENNY breaks away. She turns around and hits him in the chest with her palms.*

JENNY: I can't! I can't, Carl! You know what Brandon said to me?! My little boy?! Five years old! He says, "Good, I'm glad! Now Grandpa can have a job again!" I don't even know where to begin on telling him how wrong that is…how wicked it is to say something like that! But the entire time I'm thinking to myself…you're right Brandon. You're right. I couldn't cry one tear for those people. Not one. That's disgusting. That is absolutely disgusting. (*pause*) If I don't take you, then I'm no better than you are. I'm no better than them.

    Pause.

CARL: Let me fish. Just until the sun comes up. Then I'll go.

JENNY: Sun's not up for another twelve hours.

CARL: That's plenty of time.

JENNY: I can't wait all night.

CARL: The water's pretty cold this time of year. It won't take too long. (*silence*)

JENNY: I can't let you do that. I won't.

CARL: A lot of them want my blood, Jenny. And a lot of them want to make me a martyr. Only thing worse than prison's the spotlight. I can't do that. I can't take that kind of heat. (*CARL reels in the line*) I did what I did. Let them sort it out. (pause)

JENNY: Jesus lord. Do you know what you're asking me?

CARL: I'll be gone by sunrise.

    JENNY sits on the edge of the dock, hanging her feet over.

JENNY: No. I could lose my job. I could go to prison. My family… Matthew…

CARL: No one knows you're here. Just the two of us.

    Silence. JENNY takes the pole out of CARL's hand. She casts.

JENNY: Dad always said…there's not many good fish in the Minnesota. (*pause*) And when you do catch one…I suppose you got to let them go.

Catch and release. Back to the river where they belong. (*she reels in the line, hands the pole back to CARL. She catches his hand and removes the handcuff that hangs from CARL's wrist*)

CARL: Thank you Jenny. Thank you.

JENNY: You know what I think Carl? On the record…I think you're no better than the rest of the folks I pick up. You're a criminal. A murderer. (*she picks up a dead carp, looks at it, tosses it in the river*) Off the record…I think you're one hell of a fisherman.

> *She kisses him on the cheek, then exits up the path. CARL reels in his line, casts again.*

CARL: Twelve more hours boys. What do you say? (*pause*) Going to be a hell of a sunrise.

> *Lights fade to black.*

> *END OF PLAY*

CHAPTER 8

T-Minus Ten and Counting

Okay. Enough. I've talked about them, other people have talked about them and you've read seven. You're probably up to your ears in information and stimulation. But hopefully you're filled with inspiration as well. Now it's time to do it yourself. I want you to write a no-holds barred, off the top of your head, first draft of a ten-minute play. And while I can't be watching over your shoulder, I'll hound you from these white pages. A word of caution: if you're not into this, don't do it. It'll be a waste of your time because you'll write something that you don't really care about and no matter how good a writer you are, it shows. That's right: when you don't care about what you're writing, it's as obvious as a third eye in the middle of your forehead. But if you do want to give it a shot, let's get to it.

Before we take the smallest step forward, the first thing I want you to do is something most of us have the hardest time doing at the beginning of our work: think. So often we just want to jump to "start," a kind of not-looking-before-we're-leaping thing wherein with wild abandon we let our fingers fly across the keyboard and allow the story to magically appear. I promise you we'll get to that, but first I just want you to sit quietly and think for a moment about this: *what's something you care about*? But I mean, *really* care about? Is there something that makes you angry, sad or joyous at the very thought of it? Tired of how the world doesn't seem to care about its youth and what's happening to their dot-com brains? Are you frightened how fragile life is, and how in the tiniest instance, it can all be snuffed out? Do you look at your grandmother with adoring eyes, and long to know all that she knows? Do you look at your boyfriend and wonder what your life would have been like if you hadn't spilled your coffee all over a then-stranger in your local diner? Are there questions about life burning in you somewhere to be answered? Is there some idea, some mystery you've always wanted to explore?

You have to write from a place in your heart where you can touch something that you really care about. Yeah, I know, you want to write a rip-roaring comedy; still, underneath it all, there has to be something that you want to say: divorce sucks, love hurts, Europe's over-rated cause the ol' US of A is where it happens if it's worth happening. I say to my students: jello in is jello out. If you don't really care about what you're writing, neither will I. Think back on the six playwrights whose work you read in this book; re-read their own thoughts of how they began writing what they wrote. They all wrote from a place of trying to understand something that was a question, curiosity or passion for them. So if you've thought of your own question, curiosity or passion that gets your juices flowing, let's get started. If you haven't, go to the gym and lift a couple of hundred pounds over your head. At least that'll be somewhat productive.

This is going to feel a little disjointed at first, but stick with it – it'll all blend together at the end. Okay, we're going to count this down like the take-off it is:

TEN:

Grab a pad of paper, or use your computer – whatever. Write in big letters the focus of your question/curiosity/passion, like: "WHAT DOES SUCCESS MEAN TO ME?" or "I LOVE THE UNEXPECTED," or, "I'M LOOKING FOR LOVE IN ALL THE WRONG PLACES." Keep this in the back of your mind the whole time you're writing; maybe it'll show up somewhere, maybe it won't. But if you focus on it, it'll be there, rumbling underneath all you say and do.

NINE:

Make up a person with an identity. Do it quick. Don't think much about it yet. Say something to yourself like, "I want to write an artist – a painter." Now make something up that the artist/painter really *wants*, really *needs* in his big life story: success, recognition, money. Now give him a real *reason* that he needs what he needs: he's been painting for twelve years and has gotten nowhere and he's losing his confidence. He can't even think of what he'd do if he weren't a painter.

Now stop: that's all you need to do for the moment on the artist. Yeah, I know. It feels all superficial and contrived at this point, but you'll layer it soon enough.

Part two: think of two, three or four other characters in the same, exact quick way you thought of the artist. Like your central character, they all should want or need something in their lives in a significant way. Make it up if you have to. Don't try to make sense of it now. Just let something fly out of our imagination and onto the page. You can change it later if it doesn't fit the story of your play.

EIGHT:

It can be drudgery, I know, but spend just an hour fleshing out all of your characters with micro-biographies. I promise you, it won't be wasted time. Think about where they grew up, what their family life was like, where and how they were educated or *if* they were formally educated. What religion do they believe in, if at all? What are their politics? What are their passions? Have they ever been in love? How many times? What are their weird, eccentric, secret quirks they don't want anyone to find out? Most importantly, what do they want or need right now, and why do they need it? Write all of this down. Don't try to make it sound pretty or resemble something you'd hand in to your English professor. Just let the thoughts flow. But do write it down; it's more concrete then.

SEVEN:

Finesse the characters. Now, bend and shape what you've thought in such a way that you can see the two, three or four characters in the same space at the same time with your central character that seems logical. What would allow that? What circumstance could bring them together? What twist of fate, chance meeting or innocent collision of their worlds will best focus back on the central character and whether that person will get what they want in this story or not? If I'm using the example above of my painter who really wants and needs recognition, maybe I give him a wife who needs more of his attention (because she needs to feel loved), an agent who needs to get out of the art business and pursue his dream of flying (because he needs to be free of responsibility) and a best-friend who thinks he needs to join the Hair Club for Men (because he needs to feel attractive). Can you see the conflict beginning to build itself? And you haven't really even started writing yet.

SIX:

A setting. Think of an *interesting, unusual* setting for your play. Take your lead from your central character. If I use the example from above of the artist/painter, I can always set the play in his studio or an art gallery. But what if I stick him in a waiting line at the Internal Revenue Service, or at a service counter for lawn mowers at Sears & Roebuck? What do I get when I take him out of the expected, and put him in an unexpected place we usually associate with, in this case, artists? And wherever you set your play, is it some place where you can introduce your other characters with ease? Bend and shape it to make it so. Using my painter, if he's in a waiting line for the IRS, called in for who-knows-why, maybe his wife and best-friend are with him. And maybe, just maybe, his agent shows up because he's being audited somewhere in the same building.

FIVE:

Reassess everything. You've got a central character that wants/really needs something, and for the purpose of the ten-minute play, will either get it, not get it or will think of Plan B by the play's end. You've got at least one other character in the play that needs and wants something too, and if you've thought it through, can somehow can be responsible for helping or hindering the central character to get what they want. You've created an interesting setting for everyone's world to collide in, and if you've been able to just let your mind wander, you've seen the smallest kernel of conflict beginning to form.

FOUR:

Solidify the story as much as you can and be specific. Let your mind imagine all the possibilities the story could take. Toss around a lot of ideas. Play each idea out to find out what best makes sense for the characters you've created. When you settle on a semi-solid idea, make sure you're clear about it (or as much as you can be clear at this point), by writing down the simple version of the story line. It might read something like this: "This is the story of a painter who desperately needs recognition from the art world, but realizes in the course of the play that what he really needs is to be recognized – seen for what he is – by those who love him." It could also read something like this: "This is the story of a painter who, while being investigated for tax fraud by the IRS, discovers that his wife is having an affair with his best friend or his agent, or what he fears most, both." And of course, there's every variation in between and beyond these two examples. To be able to condense your story down to a simple one or two line description is a great exercise that forces you to get really clear about what you're writing.

Now take out your paper that we started this whole process with – the one that identifies your question/curiosity/passion. Think about it one more time, because it's time to start writing.

THREE:

Let's go for it. Don't get bogged down with a title – let the play inspire you later. Just start writing. Maybe you don't even know what you're going to write. That's okay. Just start writing.

Remember, the play has to have some sort of structure to it and since time is of the essence, try to start in the middle, not at the beginning. Or start at the end, and write backwards to the beginning. Do whatever you want to do, but keep the structure in the front part of your brain and don't forget that you've got to have some sort of *driving dramatic action* (the central character growing increasing more desperate to get what he wants) in the story that is complicated by other people, events beyond everyone's control or life circumstances. And as you write along, *complicate the story.* Make it seem that the obstacles that keep the central character from getting what they want are almost insurmountable.

Here's the coach in me: Now take us on a ride! Let us think we're going in one direction and surprise us when you shift to another! Write the unexpected! Surprise us! Don't let me predict what's going to happen – that's boring. BORING! Keep us guessing what's going to happen next. Go, go, go! Don't be afraid to write too much. You can cut it back later. STOP THINKING! Just write. Write until you have to stop. So what if you've only written three pages. Who cares? You'll write three more pages tomorrow. Do what you can, then pat yourself on the back.

TWO:

Finish the play. As muddy, confused, stupid, uninteresting, lame and vile as you think it is, just finish the play. Don't go over what you've already written, just finish the play. Force yourself; it's the only way for you to know what you have and don't have to play with when you get down to the real skill of writing: rewriting.

ONE:

You've got the first draft of a play. Congratulations. Yeah, I know you think it sucks. But now you have a chance to make it better. Answer all of these questions in your next rewrite:

1. Did I make it clear in the story that the central character wants something? Is the conflict clear?

2. Did I create enough obstacles that get in the way of the central character getting what s/he wants?

3. Is there a structure to the story that pushes the dramatic action forward, causing one event to lead to the next?

4. Is there any way that I can deepen or layer the characters? Can I give them behaviors that will make them both interesting and engaging to an audience? Is there something from their biographies that I can bring into the story that will add texture?

5. Is there something theatrical about the story? Am I using all the dramatic possibilities that a stage, live actors, lighting, sound, scenery and costumes can afford?

6. Do the characters sound different or do they all sound the same? Can I better use language to indicate their characters?

7. Is there anything that I'm being stubborn about that doesn't belong in the story, but that I like anyway and should cut now before I become too attached to it?

8. Do I address in the play what I was passionate about before I started writing, no matter how subtle?

BLAST OFF

What can you say now? You can say you've written a ten-minute play, IF you've edited down your work to ten pages. Is it good? Is it interesting? Is it engaging? Well, you probably won't know that for a while until you've reshaped the play five times over, brought more and more of your voice into its making, and then seen it read with actors, and if you're lucky, an audience. But at least you began something and are no longer carrying around an idea that you've had in your head for the last three years. Now go do something nice for yourself. We should always celebrate what seem to be even our smallest victories. Blast off, baby.

If you're a writer, that's what you do. You can't bake a pan of lasagna and call it a play.

~ Me, from The Playwrights Survival Guide

CHAPTER 9

Ten Last Thoughts

No fanfare; here they are:

1. There is something so unique and precious about you – you as a person, writer, friend and companion. Don't lose that in your writing. It's what makes your special and different. Don't try to be someone else's idea of a writer. Be yourself. That's what I want to see in your writing.

2. You're the only person that can write your play with the vision that you have of the story. Listen to what others have to say; take in their advice. But don't write anyone's version of your play but yours. A play written by committee is hardly a play at all.

3. Learn the difference between when your ego is listening to criticism and when you writer's heart and soul is. If you're unsure of yourself, ask a friend you trust to tell you when your ego's getting in the way.

4. Write from the heart, not from the head. You can't go wrong. I'll always marvel and admire you for your insight into the human condition, but I can only applaud you for turning a witty phrase.

5. When in doubt, read. Read as many plays, books about playwrights and books about the theatre as you can find. Learn from the people who've been there, are there and are looking to stay there. They've got something important to share.

AND ON THE TEN-MINUTE PLAY:

6. Ten minutes is ten pages, *maximum*. Cheating gets you nowhere you want to be.

7. Remember, somebody has to eventually produce what you've written, so be sensible.

8. A ten-minute play has all the good dramatic elements that a longer play has.

9. Care about what you're writing about; it shows up even in a ten-minute play.

10. Once you've mastered this form, go on to the next. We need writers in the theatre that can write longer-length plays.

Any questions or comments about *A More Perfect 10: Writing (and Producing) the Ten-Minute Play?* Contact the author at his website: www.garygarrison.com, or through the Dramatists Guild of America at ggarrison@dramatistsguild.com. Production and performance permissions for each play cited in the book must be secured from the individual playwright. Contact me, if interested, and I'll put you in touch with the playwright.

Sample Title Page

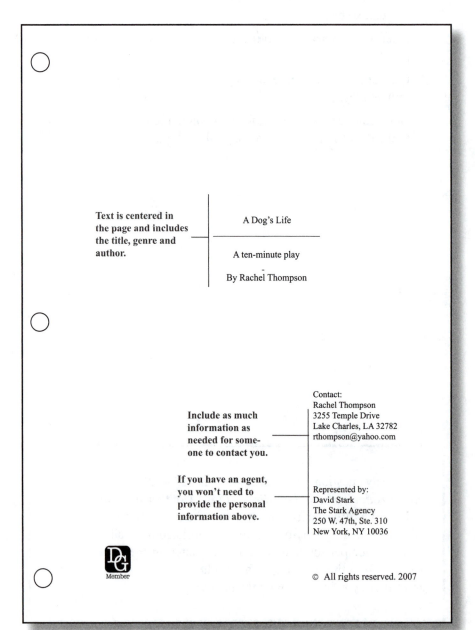

Text is centered in the page and includes the title, genre and author.

A Dog's Life

A ten-minute play

By Rachel Thompson

Include as much information as needed for someone to contact you.

Contact:
Rachel Thompson
3255 Temple Drive
Lake Charles, LA 32782
rthompson@yahoo.com

If you have an agent, you won't need to provide the personal information above.

Represented by:
David Stark
The Stark Agency
250 W. 47th, Ste. 310
New York, NY 10036

Traditional Play Format

From Tennessee Williams' *Not About Nightingales*

Essential page numbering**
16.

Dialogue begins 1.5 inches from left side to account for binding. Dialogue is single-spaced.

                    BOSS
               (removes cover from basket)
Speak of biscuits and what turns up but a nice batch of
homemade cookies! Have one young lady - Jim boy!

               (Jim takes two.)

Stage action is indented 3 inches from left; put in parenthesis. A blank line is inserted before and after.

                    BOSS
Uh-huh, you've got an awful big paw, Jimmy!
                 (laughs)
Show the new Arky-what's-it to Miss Daily news - or is it
the Morning Star? Have a chair! I'll be right with you -
                 (vanishes for a moment)
Sweat, sweat, sweat's all I do these hot breezy days!

Dialogue extends to 1.0 inch from right margin

                    JIM
                 (sotto voce)
He thinks you're a newspaper woman.

Stage action reliant on the proceeding dialogue is indented to the left of the character name.

                    BOSS
Turn on that fan.
                 (emerging)
Well, now, let's see -

                    EVA
To begin with I'm not -

Character name in all caps; in the center of the page.

                    BOSS
You've probably come here to question me about that ex-
convicts story in that damned yellow sheet down there in
Wilkes county - That stuff about getting Pellagra in here
- Jimmy, hand me that sample menu!

Standard font for this formatting is 12.0 point, Courier New.

                    JIM
She's not a reporter.

                    BOSS
Aw. - What is your business, young lady?

Stage action is indented 3.0 inches from left margin and enclosed in parentheses.

                 (She opens her purse and spills
                  contents on floor.)

**There are many ways to paginate your play, from the straightforward numerical sequence of 1, 2, 3 to an older format of I-2-16, (meaning Act 1, Scene 2, Page 16).

Modern Play Format

From Tennessee Williams' *Not About Nightingales*

Essential page
numbering
16.

BOSS
You've probably come here to question me about that ex-convicts story in that damned
yellow sheet down there in Wilkes county – That stuff about getting Pellagra in here
– Jimmy, hand me that sample menu!

Dialogue begins
1.5 inches from
left side to
account for
binding. Dialogue
is single-spaced.

JIM
She's not a reporter.

Character name
in all caps; in the
center of the page.

BOSS
Aw. – What is your business, young lady?

EVA
I understand there's a vacancy here. Mr. McBurney, my landlady's brother-in-law,
told her that you were needing a new stenographer and I'm sure that I can qualify
for the position. I'm a college graduate, Mr. Whalen, I've had three years of business
experience – references with me – but, oh – I've – I've had such abominable luck
these last six months. – the last place I worked – the business recession set in they
had to cut down on their sales-force – they gave me a wonderful letter – I've got in
with me.

Dialogue extends
to 1.0 inch from
right margin

She opens her purse and spills contents
on floor.

Stage action begins
in the center of the
page and scans to
the right margin. A
blank line is inserted
before and after.

BOSS
Anybody outside?

EVA
Yes. That woman.

Standard font for
this formatting is
12.0 point, New
Times Roman.

BOSS
What woman?

EVA
The one from Wisconsin. She's still waiting –

BOSS
I told you I don't want to see her.
              (talking into phone)
How's the track, Bert? Fast? Okay.

Stage action reliant
on the proceeding
dialogue is indented
to the left of the
character name.

Sailor Jack's mother, MRS. BRISTOL, has
quietly entered. She carries a blanket.

MRS. BRISTOL
I beg your pardon, I – You see I'm Jack Bristol's mother, and I've been wanting to
have a talk with you so long about – about my boy!